FAMINE ASPECTS OF BENGAL DISTRICTS

FAMINE ASPECTS OF BENGAL DISTRICTS.

BY

W. W. HUNTER, B.A., LL.D.

GYAN

Published by

Gyan Publishing House
5, Ansari Road
Daryaganj, New Delhi-110002
Phone: 011-47034999, 9811692060
E-mail: books@gyanbooks.com

Distribution Network
gyanbooks.com
India, USA, Canada, UK, Australia

ISBN: 978-81-212-5557-8 (HB)
First Published, 1873

2nd Impression 2024

Printed at: Gyan Press, Delhi.

FAMINE ASPECTS OF BENGAL DISTRICTS
Author: W. W. HUNTER

FAMINE ASPECTS OF BENGAL DISTRICTS.

FAMINE ASPECTS OF BENGAL DISTRICTS.

BY

W. W. HUNTER, B.A., LL.D.,

DIRECTOR-GENERAL OF STATISTICS TO THE GOVERNMENT OF INDIA.

LONDON:
TRÜBNER & CO., 57 & 59 LUDGATE HILL.
1874.

CONTENTS.

DISTRICT ACCOUNTS.

ENGLISH EQUIVALENTS.

Harvests.—There are four chief harvests in the agricultural year.

1. The *Aus* rice, sown broadcast in April or May, reaped in August or September.
2. The *Aman* rice (the great harvest of the year), sown broadcast in lowlands in April, May, and June; planted out on highlands in June or July; reaped in November and December.
3. The *Boro* rice, sown broadcast in October, reaped in March.
4. The *Rabi*, or spring crops, consisting of peas, pulses, oilseeds, and miscellaneous green crops, sown in October, reaped in February.

Weights.—The statutary *seer* is 2·205 lbs.; the bazar *seer* 2 lbs. But as a matter of fact the local seers still vary from 1½ to 2½ lbs., I have reduced them to one standard. To convert the weights in the following pages into avoirdupois, multiply the seers by 2 to find the pounds, and the maunds by 82 to find the pounds—*i.e.*, 2 lbs. = 1 *seer*; 82 lbs. = 1 *maund*.

Land Measures.—The statutary *bigha* is 14,400 square feet, and I have reduced the local *bighas* of the various Districts to this standard. The *bigha* is therefore ⅓ of an acre. To find acres, multiply the *bighas* by 3; 640 acres make a square mile.

Money.—A rupee for all practical purposes in small calculations may be taken as two shillings; and an anna as three-halfpence, or 1·16th of a rupee.

Prices.—The rate of rice is expressed either by so many rupees and annas the maund, or more commonly by so many seers per rupee. The following table exhibits the price per maund expressed by the seers per rupee:—

Seers per Re.	Price per Md.	Seers per Re.	Price per Md.	Seers per Re.	Price per Md.	Seers per Re.	Price per Md.
1	Rs. 40 0 0	11	Rs. 3 10 2	21	Rs. 1 14 5	31	Rs. 1 3 4
2	,, 20 0 0	12	,, 3 5 4	22	,, 1 13 1	32	,, 1 4 0
3	,, 13 5 4	13	,, 3 1 3	23	,, 1 11 10	33	,, 1 3 4
4	,, 10 0 0	14	,, 2 13 8	24	,, 1 10 8	34	,, 1 2 9
5	,, 8 0 0	15	,, 2 10 8	25	,, 1 9 7	35	,, 1 2 3
6	,, 6 10 8	16	,, 2 8 0	26	,, 1 8 7	36	,, 1 1 9
7	,, 5 11 5	17	,, 2 5 1	27	,, 1 7 8	37	,, 1 1 3
8	,, 5 0 0	18	,, 2 3 6	28	,, 1 6 10	38	,, 1 0 10
9	,, 4 7 1	19	,, 2 1 8	29	,, 1 6 1	39	,, 1 0 5
10	,, 4 0 0	20	,, 2 0 0	30	,, 1 5 4	40	,, 1 0 0

FAMINE ASPECTS OF BENGAL DISTRICTS.

WHEN engaged in the famine-stricken Districts in 1866, it seemed to me that the suddenness, and to some extent the uncontrollable character, of that calamity proceeded from want of knowledge on four points. In the first place, no information existed as to what the rise in prices after the winter rice harvest really meant. Every one felt that it betokened scarcity during the coming year, but no evidence was available by which to gauge its full and terrible significance. In the second place, a most embarrassing diversity of opinion disclosed itself as to the point at which famine prices would be reached. Some District Officers believed that their people could manage to keep themselves alive when grain was selling at prices which, as a matter of fact, proved to be starvation rates. Nor, thirdly, had the relative value of the four harvests of the year been accurately realised, or the function which they severally discharge in feeding the population. People knew that the December rice harvest (*aman*) was the great crop of the year. But few adequately appreciated the impossibility of making up for its loss by the produce of the preceding September harvest (*aus*), or of the green crops (*rabi*) in the following spring or by the early rice crop (*boro*). This question was complicated by the fact that the relative importance of the four harvests (as food-suppliers) varies in different parts of Bengal. In the fourth place, the position of each District as regards its means of importation from without, and of distribution within its own area, had never been systematically studied. Roads, rivers, and railways (more than State charity or Relief Works) constitute the machinery of mitigation during a famine. They tend to place the food stores of the whole Province at the disposal of its most afflicted parts, to equalise the calamity down to a bearable level, and to avert that local isolation which, in 1866, reduced Orissa to the state of a dismasted ship at sea without provisions. Some Districts have very inadequate means either for external importation or internal distribution. Some have facilities for the one but not for the other. Several Districts can only obtain supplies from without, before the setting in of the monsoon; others are practically cut off during the rains; while in many the rainy months greatly multiply the channels of transit. The proper season for throwing relief into a District varies according to its geographical position and its deltaic or fluvial phenomena; and once that season has passed, subsequent efforts come too late.

EFFORTS TO OBTAIN INFORMATION.—Accordingly in 1869, while collecting the materials for my Statistical Account of Bengal, it seemed well that accurate information should be placed on record with regard to these four points. After a series of questions regarding the three ordinary forms of natural calamity, namely, Blights, Floods, and Droughts, and with respect to the compensating influences of the two latter on high and low levels, I addressed the following inquiries to each of the fifty-eight District Officers of Bengal:—

Of Famines.—"Please give, in as few sentences as possible, an account of the famine of 1866 in your District, its local causes and severity, with the maximum price reached, and a statement showing the monthly returns of prices from its beginning to its close. In most Districts this period should be considered to embrace the sixteen months from September 1st, 1865, to January 1st, 1867; but if you have not the earlier returns, please leave the spaces blank. Have the local prices in your District returned to what were considered their ordinary rates before the famine? Different ideas are entertained as to the point at which scarcity amounts to famine, but for political and financial purposes, this point may be taken to be that at which Government relief operations become necessary, that is to say, when in order to save the people from starvation, the State has to find work and food (or wages) for the able-bodied, and to give food in charity to those who are incapable of labour. Assuming this to be the point at which famine begins, please consider carefully at what point prices may be held to have reached famine rates in your District. In Districts where grain is ordinarily very cheap, this point may be reached by a much lower rate than in Districts where the people are accustomed to high prices. But after due consideration of this and other circumstances, state the rates of paddy, or whatever is your staple grain, at which you think that relief operations become necessary, and give your reasons; your attention is particularly directed to this subject. State also what you would consider as warnings of famine in your District. Such warnings may be either the loss of the crops or a serious rise in prices after the December (*áman*) harvest is reaped. Give the rates which, if reached in January or February, you would consider a warning of a famine later in the year. Does your District depend chiefly on the *aus* or the *aman* harvest? and could the first make up for an almost total loss of the second, and enable the people to live through the year without actual famine? In conclusion, do you think that the means at the disposal of your District are at present sufficient to avert the extremity of famine by importation from other parts? These means are harbours, railways, roads, rivers, and canals. Do you think they afford sufficient facilities for importation to prevent danger of isolation of any particular parts of your District in time of famine? After considering the event of 1866, have you any local suggestions to offer as regards remedial or mitigating measures during famine for your District?" *

NECESSITY FOR A FAMINE SYSTEM. — The replies received to this inquiry form a valuable body of evidence as to the famine aspects of Bengal. If Government is to deal adequately with a scarcity, it must take action at or just after the December harvest. But a famine does not actually develop itself till several months later, and Indian Governors have hitherto shrunk from a vast outlay in December with a view to avert a possible calamity next May. In the absence of well-tested evidence, it could only be a matter of guesswork whether a famine will or will not take place. This element of the unknown contained within it infinite hopes and chances of escape. Who could tell whether the existing grain stocks in the country, private importations, the diminished consumption caused by high prices,

* Question No. 12 of the Fourth or Agricultural Series, printed *in extenso* at pp. lx., lxi. of my plan for an Imperial Gazetteer of India, 1870.

and the spring crops, might not tide the people over to the next September harvest, without absolute famine? There might be cause for grave anxiety; but the history of past scarcities proves that Indian administrators decline to spend public money in the cold weather, on the chance of a famine which after all may not take place in spring. No systematised materials existed on which a safe forecast could be based.

BASIS OF SUCH A SYSTEM. — The Returns which I collected from the District Officers supplied the basis which was thus required. Many of them I verified by personally visiting the Districts to which they refer; others were checked by means of official and private correspondence. While deficient in several points, they approach sufficiently near to a formulated system of Famine Warnings, as to warrant the Government to take action in time to avert the full bitterness of famine. Considered along with the price-currents and the events of the season, they place in a clear light the chances of the coming year; and furnish the evidence on which to decide whether those chances are sufficient to justify an outlay of public money, and the timely organisation of Relief Works in anticipation of famine.

Accordingly, on the failure of the present winter harvest being ascertained (October 1873), I submitted a portion of them to the Viceroy, and it was considered desirable that the whole should be rendered available without delay. The following pages condense such information as I possess regarding forty Districts, with a population of fifty million souls. They start with the northern Divisions of Patná and Bhágalpur, in which famine is now most imminent, and proceed District by District down the valley of the Ganges to the seaboard. I have not deemed it necessary to swell the work by similar statistics for the three eastern Divisions of Dacca, Chittagong, and Assam, as those parts of Bengal have hitherto enjoyed a practical immunity from famine. I was also asked to estimate the agricultural and labouring population of each District.

A system of Famine Warnings such as I have endeavoured to frame, deals with ten separate subjects. In the first place, it shows the highest price of rice and other food grains in each District, during the only great famine which has been accurately recorded; namely, that of 1866. Second, The price at which, in the opinion of the responsible officer in charge of the District, famine rates are reached, and at which scarcity arrives at the point of actual famine. Third, The price of rice which, if reached after the December harvest or in January or February, ought to be accepted as a warning of famine later in the year. Fourth, The functions and relative importance of the three chief harvests, as the food-suppliers of the District. Many Districts depend almost wholly on the December or *aman* rice; in a few the September or *aus* rice would enable the people to live through the year without absolute famine; in others, the spring crops (*rabi*) form an important supplement to the rice harvest. Fifth, The are aunder cultivation, the out-turn of the crops, and the yield per acre, so far as the absence of rural statistics in Lower Bengal renders it possible to form any estimate. Sixth, Means of transit and facilities for the importation and distribution of food in time of scarcity. This head includes roads, rivers, canals, harbours, railways, channels, amd all other means of communication, whether natural or artificial; the risk of isolation to which any individual part of the District may be liable; and such proposals as the responsible officer in charge may have to offer with a view to averting this risk. Seventh, Remedial or mitigating measures in time of famine, which the local experience of District Officers may suggest; such as public works or relief centres for distributing food, and the special inability of any particular classes of the District population to bear the strain of famine. Eighth, The agricultural population who actually hold the plough, or are engaged in tending cattle; and who would come within the class which is seriously affected by a famine. Ninth, The labouring population and poorer sorts of craftsmen, who in like manner would come within reach of want during a famine. Tenth, The total of these two classes, with a summary of the total population of the District.

The following pages deal with these ten points so far as my materials permit, under each of the forty Districts. They involve many details which have to be separately considered, and which cannot be reduced to a tabular statement.

Tabulated Famine Warnings.—But several of the main features of the system are capable of being exhibited in this form. Thus, the famine prices and population estimates can be shown at a glance in a tabular shape. In fixing the point at which actual famine begins, I have entered into no abstract theories as to the relation of scarcity to starvation, but adopted the easily-understood principle, that when the people cannot live without relief works, or state charity, the famine point for all administrative purposes is reached.

With regard to the food prices which ought to be accepted as a warning of famine in the coming year, it should be remembered that such rates, although affording a valuable warning, do not form an absolute criterion.

The Districts of Bengal do not depend in equal degrees upon the December harvest. In some of them (as in the two afflicted Divisions of Patná and Bhágalpur) the spring crops form an important subsidiary source of the food supply. In other Divisions further down the Gangetic Valley, these spring crops largely consist of oil-seeds or articles of export, and are devoted rather to paying the rent than to the supply of food-grains. In the same way, in different Districts the September rice harvest performs a function of very different importance. There are, moreover, several parts of the country, such as the hill tracts, in which rice is not the staple food of the people; and there are some in which it is so seldom bought or sold as to render its market rates a merely fanciful criterion with regard to the food supply of the people. Above all, the certainty and value of such a tabular statement are affected by the fact that no great scarcity runs precisely the same course as its predecessor. The main features of Bengal famines follow a common type, but do not exactly repeat themselves.

But in spite of these and similar reservations (which will be suggested in detail under each District in the following pages), a tabulated system of famine warnings will be found to have a practical value. The returns were drawn up at a time when the calamity of 1866 was still fresh in the memory of the District Officers. In the two northern Divisions, indeed, the officers were able to compare the teachings of that famine with those of the milder scarcity of 1868-69. Nor were their calculations affected, as they might possibly be at the present crisis, by the perturbing influences incident to a year of impending famine.

The following table proves that the experience of 1866 has been carefully utilised in the preparation of the

Returns. Allowing for the different circumstances of each District, the figures disclose a surprising unanimity, both as to what rates in January should be accepted as a warning of famine, and as to the point at which actual famine is reached. With the exception of the Orissa and Kuch Behar Divisions, whose circumstances are peculiar, the District average of each of the other six Divisions (comprising 32 Districts) only varies from Rs. 2-6 to Rs. 2-10 as the price of rice per maund which, if reached in January, forms a warning of famine later in the year. The same remarkable *consensus* is disclosed as to the point at which prices amount to actual famine, and at which Relief Works should begin. In the two great adjoining Divisions above the delta (Patná and Bhágalpur), with their twelve Districts and 19¾ million inhabitants, the District average Famine Rate is precisely the same, viz., Rs. 3-14 per maund for common rice. The three adjacent Divisions of the delta (Rájsháhí, Bardwán, and the Presidency), with their fifteen Districts and 22 million inhabitants, exhibit an equal uniformity. Famine warnings in the two northern adjoining ones average Rs. 2-10 for rice in January; and in the three, the actual Famine Rate varies only from Rs. 4-1 to Rs. 4-4 for common rice per maund. In Orissa, the people are poorer, the purchasing power of silver is greater, and the returns give (as they ought to give) a lower price both for the point of famine warning and for that of actual famine rates. Kuch Behar, the other exceptional Division, has hitherto been exempt from famine, and no materials exist for a well-founded forecast of famine rates. Indeed, throughout the hill tracts of this Division rice is scarcely brought into the market at all.

TABULATED SYSTEM OF FAMINE WARNINGS.

I.		II.	III.	IV.	V.	VI.	VII.	VIII.
Name of Division.	Number of Districts.	Total Population.	Agricultural Population.	Labourers and poorer Craftsmen.	Total Agriculturists and Labourers, III. and IV.	Highest price of Rice per maund in 1866.	Famine prices. Rice per maund; District Average.	Famine Warnings. Rice per maund in January; District Average.
Patná	6	13,122,743	7,202,661	2,986,419	10,189,080	Av. Rs. 5-4½	Av. Rs. 2-14	Av. Rs. 2-7
Bhágalpur	6	6,613,358	3,217,839	2,041,767	5,259,606	„ „ 5-8	„ „ 3-14	„ „ 2-9
Rájsháhí	7	8,893,738	5,384,868	1,761,654	7,146,522	„ „ 4-10	„ „ 4-4	„ „ 2-10
Kuch Behar	5	1,533,656	*612,540	*126,105	*738,645	„ „ 5-8	„ „ 5-1	„ „ 3-5
Chota Nágpur	5	3,825,571	2,084,484	876,210	2,960,694	„ „ 5-1	„ „ 4-8	„ „ 2-8
Bardwán	5	7,237,981	3,517,839	2,072,541	5,590,380	„ „ 6-2	„ „ 4-1	„ „ 2-10
Presidency	3	†5,338,953	2,876,958	1,450,812	4,327,770	„ „ 4-14	„ „ 4-2	„ „ 2-6
Orissa	3	3,034,690	1,394,793	707,247	2,102,040	„ „ 10-1	„ „ 3-8	„ „ 2-3
Total	40	50,150,690	26,291,982	12,022,755	38,314,737	Av. Rs. 5-14-0	Av. Rs. 4-2-0	Av. Rs. 2-9-6

* No details of population are given for Kuch Behar proper and the Gáro Hills.

† Exclusive of Calcutta, the suburbs and the shipping.

Basis of Population Estimates.—I shall presently give a tabular statement showing each of the Districts in detail. Meanwhile it is necessary to make some remarks regarding the population columns. These columns are intended to show the number of agriculturists, labourers, and poorer sorts of craftsmen who would be seriously affected by a famine. Such an enumeration in Bengal may be made upon two distinct principles; the first according to Castes, the second according to Occupation. Several sources of error are inherent to both methods. The Caste Statements show only the Hindus and aborigines, while in several Districts the Muhammadans form more than half the total population, and in all they constitute a considerable proportion of it. Moreover, the Caste Statements include only Hindus under "the Agricultural and Pastoral Castes," while the aboriginal races and semi-Hinduised aborigines have to be shown as labourers. But as a matter of fact, a large proportion of the aborigines and semi-aboriginal Castes are cultivators, although they form the lowest class of husbandmen, and on the approach of famine abandon their fields, or migrate and are thrown on the mass of the labouring population. According to the "Agricultural and Pastoral Castes," the full number of cultivators is seldom shown; while in some cases, the return of the labouring classes, according to my Caste Statements, exceeds the truth, as it includes aborigines and the semi-aboriginal communities.

The error in the returns derived from the Occupation Statement of the Census, is more delicate. It arises from the two facts that a very large proportion of the labourers are also small husbandmen on their own account, and that it is almost impossible to draw the line in India between the artisan and the labouring classes. No amount of statistical acumen can get rid of the first source of error, and my figures must be accepted as subject to it. I have done my best to eliminate the second. In my enumeration of the cultivators according to occupation, I have deducted all those who are tenure-holders belonging to classes who do not usually hold the plough with their own hands. I have also deducted the more substantial of the classes who live by tending animals, such as elephant-keepers, buffalo-dealers, cattle-merchants, jockeys, &c. Such men are generally well off, and do not come within reach of hunger during famines. They form the "excepted classes" which I deduct from the total cultivating population, in each of the separate District Accounts. In the same way I have eliminated from the labouring population all artisans who can be trusted to live through a famine without risk of distress or want. Thus, I have excepted the jute-spinners, who are generally well off; while I have included the cotton-spinners and cotton-weavers, who in many Districts succumb. As a matter of fact the weavers of Jahánábád, then in Húglí District, formed one of the most hopeless communities with whom we had to deal during the famine of 1866. Like many similar guilds in Bengal, their craft had decayed before the ever-rising tide of English importations, and the strain of famine prices sufficed to give the last stroke to their ruin. Again, while the fishing and boating castes have to be included as an entity in the Caste Statement, I include only the boatmen as labourers in the Occupation Statement. The Caste Census gives them undivided, so I cannot separate them according to the caste principle of enumeration. But in reality the fishermen get on very well during a famine, while the boating castes who are engaged in the conveyance of goods are thrown out of employment by the general stagnation of trade, and compelled either to abandon their usual work and live as fishermen of a less skilled sort, or to have recourse to charity, or to temporarily migrate. The personal servants, according to the Caste Statement, include all engaged in menial employment, without minute details as to office. But according to the Occupation Statements, I have been able to exclude cooks, and all other servants whose position places them beyond reach of actual famine. A critical examination will suggest several difficulties of the same sort. I only ask it to be believed that each of these difficulties has been carefully considered by the light of the experience afforded by the famine of 1866, and that the safest view has in each case been adopted. Finally, in order to find the total population according to occupation, I have multiplied the male adults by three. That is to say, I have assumed that to each man or youth of a working age, there are a woman and one other person below the working age. In some Districts this proportion seems to me to be too high; in others too low. But after very careful examination, I find it on the whole to be nearer to the truth than by multiplying the male adults either by two or by four.

Classes liable to Famine.—With a view to placing the facts in the clearest light, and to supplying the means of verification and of testing my figures, I have, under each District, given six separate calculations. First, the agriculturists according to castes; second, the total according to occupation; third, according to occupation after the deduction of the "excepted classes;" fourth, the number *actually employed in cultivation*, both the male adults and the total obtained by multiplying them by three; fifth, the labourers according to the Caste Statement of the Census; sixth, the labourers and poorer craftsmen according to the Occupation Statements. The statistics at present available do not permit me to attempt a more exact precision.

The letter of instructions asking me to attempt these estimates, explained that I would "not be able to give absolutely accurate answers; the nearest approximation must suffice."

The returns obtained from the Occupation Statements of the Census approach nearest the truth. I have therefore selected them for the preceding and the following tabular statements. They exhibit 38⅓ millions of labourers and agriculturists, out of a total population of 50 millions included in the 40 Districts,* or three-fourths of the whole population.

It would be beyond my knowledge to say what proportion of these labourers and agriculturists are within reach of starvation during a famine. But the following rough estimate may be useful. I consider that 9½ millions, or one-fourth of them, do not earn more than Rs. 5 (ten shillings) a month, or say 3 annas a day, during a working month of 27 days; another quarter of them earn between Rs. 5 and Rs. 8 (*i.e.*, between ten shillings and sixteen shillings) a month. The earnings of another quarter of them may be put down between Rs. 8 and Rs. 10-8 (*i.e.*, sixteen to twenty-one shillings) a month. The remaining quarter averages about Rs. 12-8 a month (twenty-five shillings), and very few even of this comfortable class can afford to spend over Rs. 16 (or thirty-two shillings) per mensem.

* Exclusive of the Garo Hills and Kuch Behar, for which no details according to occupation exist.

It is not my business here to make proposals as to the methods of dealing with the famine, but merely to furnish a basis of systematised evidence by which such proposals may be judged. Elsewhere I have had an opportunity of submitting any views I may personally entertain with regard to the main lines of a Famine Policy. For the present it suffices merely to summarise the evidence contained in the following District Accounts.

First.—Ordinary Prices. The rate of common rice in prosperous years may be set down at 30 seers for the rupee, or Rs. 1-5 a maund, or say 1½ farthings per pound.

Second.—Famine Warnings. When rice reaches double these rates after the December harvest, or in January or February, that is to say, to 15 seers per rupee, Rs. 2-10 a maund, or 3 farthings per pound; these prices should be accepted as a warning of famine later in the year, and would justify action in anticipation of famine; unless the facilities for importation, or some other of the special conditions mentioned in the District Accounts, rendered famine unlikely in the District.

Third.—Actual Famine Rates. If rice rises to three times the ordinary rates in prosperous years, that is to say, to 10 seers per rupee, or Rs. 4 a maund, or 5 farthings per pound, the actual famine point is in some Districts of Bengal reached, and Relief Works become in such Districts necessary. This formula must also be taken as subject to the limitations and reservations contained in the District Accounts. Different localities exhibit very different powers of resistance to the strain of famine; but so far as it is possible to reduce the experience of the District Officers to a tabular statement, it may be represented thus :—

PRICE OF COMMON RICE.

	Per rupee.	*Per maund.*	*Per lb.*
a. In prosperous years	30 seers	Rs. 1 5	1½ farthings.
b. Famine warnings in January	15 „	2 10	3 „
c. Actual famine	10 „	4 0	5 „

Fourth.—These figures very forcibly suggest the extremely small difference (when expressed in English money) between plenty and scarcity. Three and a half farthings per pound represent the whole intermediate area between a year of prosperity and one of famine; while there are only two farthings per pound between the rates which amount to a famine warning and those at which the famine point is reached.

Fifth.—These facts explain the invariable and urgent demand by the native community, to prohibit exportation during famine. I would not be understood to advocate that demand. Such a measure involves wide considerations of public policy which cannot be discussed here. But I have never seen the question adequately discussed by the light which these figures now shed upon it. I am told that the retail price of rice in Europe may rise a few farthings a pound without causing anything like a sudden cessation of the consumption. But in Bengal two farthings make the whole difference between a famine warning and the famine point, and three and a half farthings per pound the whole difference between a time of plenty and a time of famine. It is clear, therefore, that as a difference of a few farthings does not cause a cessation of the demand in Europe, exportation will go on although these same few farthings may mean starvation for the Bengal peasant.

Actual experience proves that export of rice is checked but not stopped by a rise of rates to famine prices. Toulmin's Weekly Circular shows an annual average export of rice from Calcutta for the 10 years ending December 31st, 1872, of 9 million maunds.* It shows that during the year of extreme famine, 1866, the exportation only dropped to 5 million of maunds, and the average of the three years, 1865-66-67, was nearly 7½ millions. Last month (October 1873), in the presence of an impending famine, 278,944 maunds were exported. During the *ten* months of actual scarcity in 1866 (from January to October), the export of rice from Calcutta exceeded 3¾ million of maunds.

Such facts explain, and to some extent justify, the native outcry for an embargo during a scarcity. *The few farthings which signify little to the European consumer mean actual famine to the population of Bengal.* Allowing the liberal yield of seven maunds of paddy per *bigha*, or four maunds of rice per *bigha*, and twelve maunds of rice per acre, the exportations last month from Calcutta swallowed up the produce of 23,245 acres in a fruitful year, or over 50,000 acres in this unprosperous one. Even under the pressure of the terrible crisis in 1866, the exportations of rice from Calcutta represented 422,210 acres of rice-land in fruitful years; 1,688,840 acres in that year with its quarter crop, and 1,266,630 acres in this year with its one-third crop. The natives complain that with one hand we are putting a hundred thousand acres under irrigation gratis, while with the other hand we are

* Toulmin's Circular for January 10, 1873:—Total of ten years, 90,507,516 maunds; average of ditto, 9,050,751; exports in 1866, 5,066,527 maunds.

sending away the produce of $1\frac{1}{4}$ million acres, supposing exportation comes down to the level of 1866.

Fifth.—The converse cry, which is invariably raised in a time of scarcity, is, for Government importations. This demand usually proceeds from the European community, and represents the English view of the function of State interference; as an embargo on exportation represents the native view of that function. It does not fall within my present instructions to express any opinion on either of these proposals.

But it is my duty to note the very general consensus disclosed on the part of the District Officers with regard to the expediency of State importations during time of famine. Different officers lay different degrees of stress upon State interference, but the experience of 1866 seems to have convinced the whole executive body in Bengal that the ordinary operation of trade breaks down during a famine, and that State interference in some form or other is necessary to save the people from starvation. Perhaps the most sensible view is that contained in the report which the Collector of Rangpur sent to me in 1871. I have given an abstract of it at page 97, concluding with the following two sentences, and showing on the one hand the peril of premature or excessive interference by the State, and on the other the danger of refusing to interfere. "Were too much imported, prices would fall, and the confidence of the merchants might be shaken and private enterprise brought to a stop. Were there no importation at all, the scarcity might turn into famine, even for the more provident portion of the community and irretrievable disaster might ensue."

Sixth.—Relief works. The best of the District Returns lay much stress upon beginning Relief Works early. The question is simply between Relief Works commenced at the outset of a famine, and indiscriminate State Charity later in its course. The people do not die at first, but in a short time they become too weak to give any effective labour upon public works, and must either die or be fed gratuitously. Several of the District Officers insist on the evil effects of indiscriminate State Charity. They would prefer a large outlay upon public works, from the very commencement of the famine, to charitable distributions afterwards to a diminished, enfeebled, and proletariate population, even although the latter course might cost less money. On this subject, among other evidence, see the opinions of the Collector and of the District Engineer of Sháhábád, pp. 42,43.

Seventh.—Emigration and gathering the people into convenient centres *versus* Home Relief. These points have been raised by several experienced officers, but as they involve a minute and careful consideration of local details, I have not deemed it safe to attempt to deal with them in the following brief District Accounts. The migrations and movements of the Bengal population will be fully exhibited in my Statistical Account of each District, proof-sheets from the first few volumes of which have been submitted to the Viceroy.

Eighth.—Miscellaneous. I have also refrained from dealing at any length in the following brief Accounts with the details of distribution. Payment in money or by rice, Government grain stores selling below the market rates, the distribution of cooked or of uncooked food at the depots, are among the questions which can only be decided by the individual events of each famine, and by the individual circumstances of each local centre of population. The narrative of the Jahánábád weavers, in my account of Húglí District, might have been much amplified, and might have been reproduced with regard to other similar communities. The case came under my own observation in 1866. The men were utterly panic-stricken and unreasonable. They rushed towards Calcutta, leaving their wives and families in misery behind them, notwithstanding the opportunities they had of earning food at home. On the other hand, the means of earning food held out to them were unsympathetic, and made too little allowance for caste prejudice. Such questions could not be profitably discussed within the brief space allotted to the following District Accounts, and I have therefore refrained from attempting what must have been an inadequate treatment of them.

PROPORTION OF PAUPER POPULATION.—The population estimates endeavour in each District to exhibit the classes whom a famine would seriously affect. But they do not form any criterion as to the number who would be forced to seek State relief. The experience of previous scarcities proves that this latter number is very small. I subjoin a table showing the facts with regard to the Famine of 1866 in the three Districts of Orissa, and the eight most seriously affected ones of Lower Bengal. These eleven Districts have a total population of 14,800,251, and a total of agriculturists and labourers (the classes whom a famine seriously affects) of 10,964,415. Yet the largest average number in any month who obtained relief from the State was 144,059, or only 0·97 per cent. of the population. In Orissa, the highest daily number who received relief was 83,713, out of a total population of 3,034,690, or 2·75 per cent. In Balasor, the most severely affected District of Orissa, the highest number was 38,163, out of a total population of 770,232, or 4·95 per cent.

STATISTICS OF RELIEF IN 1866.

I. Districts in which the Famine of 1866 was most severely felt.	II. Total Population.	III. Labourers and Agriculturists.	IV. Highest Number of Paupers relieved daily in the months specified (Famine Commissioner's Report, ii. 637).	V. Percentage of the highest number of Paupers relieved daily in the total Population.
Nadiya	1,812,795	1,230,285	7,620, Aug.	0·42
24 Parganas	1,951,137	1,478,547	9,492, Nov.	0·48
Húglí with Howrah	1,488,556	1,045,008	7,041, Oct.	0·47
Bardwan	2,034,745	1,579,062	1,490, Aug.	0·07
Bankura	526,772	405,579	14,818, Oct.	2·81
Midnapur	2,540,963	2,026,956	9,606, Aug.	0·37
Manbhúm	995,570	763,629	9,630, Oct.	0·96
Singhbhúm	415,023	333,309	649, July–Sept.	0·15
Balasor	770,232	541,647	38,163, Sept.	4·95
Cattack	1,494,784	1,004,490	34,704, Oct.	2·32
Purí	769,674	555,903	10,846, Oct.	1·41
Total	14,800,251	10,964,415	144,059	Av. 0·97

PAUPER POPULATION IN 1866.—In estimating the significance of these figures, three points must be considered. In the first place, there is ground for reasonable hope that by timely measures the famine will be kept down at a less severe degree of pressure in 1874 than in 1866. But, in the second place, there is unhappily little doubt that the Government measures in 1866 were both tardy and inadequate. The numbers who required relief were greater than those who received it. In the third place, large bodies of people received practical relief from employment in public works who are not entered in the above return of those who were fed gratuitously.

If we examine these figures by the purchasing power of wages during a famine, we are surprised by the small number of persons who seek gratuitous relief from the State. A household of four persons, say two adults and two children, reduced to one meal a day, consume 1½ seers of rice. In order to enable the father to do his daily work, he would require a second meal of half a seer, making a total of 2 seers a day. If the daily consumption dropped below this, severe suffering would have to be endured. Now, at even the point which I take to be the beginning of famine, namely, Rs. 4 a maund, or 10 seers for the rupee, this low scale of diet would cost Rs. 6 a month. When rates rose to 8 seers for the rupee, or Rs. 5 per maund, two seers a day would cost Rs. 7-8 a month. Yet about a fourth of the families in Bengal do not earn more than Rs. 5 a month even in prosperous times. It might be expected, therefore, that a fourth of the population in famine-stricken areas would be thrown upon State relief. But at the outset of a famine the people fall back upon roots and various sorts of inferior green food. The children and weaker members of the family die, and those who survive eke out a very insufficient quantity of rice by roots and wild plants. The wages which would not suffice to feed an average family of four, are sufficient for the two or three members who survive. The rural population enters a famine as a frigate goes into battle, cleared of all useless gear and inefficient members.

The District which was most severely tried in 1866, and which also possessed an energetic and resolute Magistrate, who was determined to reduce the suffering to a minimum, was Balasor. The highest number relieved there in any month amounted to five per cent. of the population, or an average of 2.68 per cent. of the population during seven months. Allowing on the one hand for the inadequacy of the relief measures in 1866, and on the other for the greater intensity of the famine in Balasor in that year, than we have reason to expect it will be in Bengal this year, I think the following forecast might be made. The Viceroy last week declared in his speech at Agra that the population in peril of famine amounted to 24 millions. From Orissa experience, it seems that not more than 2.75 per cent. can ever be thrown upon State relief, probably much fewer. This would represent a total of 660,000 on 24 millions, to each of whom ½ a seer of rice per diem must be allowed. The monthly consumption during 30 days would be 99,000,000 seers of rice, or 247,500 maunds. If this rice can be purchased, as it seems probable that it can be timely imported, at 15 seers for the rupee, or the rate of famine warning, the total monthly cost of feeding the 660,000 pauper population would be £66,000. If this expenditure be protracted over six months (and it seems very unlikely that it will be so), the total expenditure on charitable relief would be £396,000.

This sum may be taken as the very largest estimate of the cost of gratuitous relief. In 1866, when the famine was more severe than we have reason to anticipate that it will be this year, the total expenditure, both on charitable relief and public works, was £254,689.* It can scarcely, however, be said that the relief measures of that year were adequate. Besides actual relief, Government has to contemplate the necessity of employing a large population on public works. The sum allotted from Imperial Revenue for special works in 1866 was £21,657 (Statement VIII.) Supposing that in the approaching famine, Government were five times more liberal, the total expenditure on relief works and charitable distributions would be just half a million. It must be remembered that I have taken as the basis of this calculation the *maximum* number relieved during the severest month in 1866, and used this maximum rate in the severest stricken districts of Orissa as the

* Statement No. IX. p. 642, vol. ii. of Famine Commissioner's Report.

average number to be relieved during six months throughout the whole famine area in 1874. Although the relief operations were inadequate at the beginning of the last famine, they expanded to a liberal and efficient standard before its close. In order to be safe, I assume that the maximum expansion of the relief measures in 1866 will be their average expansion in 1874. This unduly liberal estimate shows a total cost of £500,000 for Relief Works and gratuitous distribution required to deal adequately with a famine-stricken population of 24 millions.

If government can buy its rice at Rs. 2-10 a maund or 15 seers per rupee, that is at the price which I give as the Famine Warning, the cost of feeding the actual paupers will be £10 per hundred adults *per mensem;* or £100 per thousand.

This sum of half a million sterling forms only $2\frac{3}{4}$ per cent. of the revenues of the territories under the Lieutenant-Governor of Bengal.* It forms just $12\frac{1}{2}$ per cent on the single item of the Land Revenue of those territories.† If we calculate the expense on the Imperial Revenues, instead of those of the one Province in which the famine takes place, the half million which may be required for adequately dealing with the calamity, is only one per cent. of the annual income of the country. The total famine-expenditure in 1866 was £254,689. Of this sum Government only contributed £143,788 ‡ *net*, the remainder being derived from subscriptions and private charity. In 1769-70, when out

* Abstract of Imperial, Provincial, and Local Revenues, p. 161, Part 1, of Bengal Administration Report for 1871-72.

† "Current Demand" for 1871-72, £3,939,596. Para. 3 of Board of Revenue's Report, No. 362, dated 18th September 1872

‡ "Net cost to Government," as per Statement VIII. Vol. I. p. 641 of Famine Commissioners' Report.

of 30 millions of people, five in every 16 were officially admitted to have perished, only £9000 were expended on relief by Government.*

This effort to bring a great natural calamity within scope of the Budget Estimates will, perhaps, strike some persons as an unsuitable application of figures. I fully realise that a large element of uncertainty enters into such a computation. It is no more possible to predict the course of a famine than to foresee the events of a war. But an intelligent forecast of the requisite expenditure can be made in both cases.

Any well-devised effort to withdraw the subject of famines from the region of the unknown into the domain of calm administrative calculation is of value. Personally, I believe that less money will suffice than the half million indicated by the foregoing estimate. More than £100,000 may be spent on public works, but much less than £400,000 on State charity. But while it is possible to calculate the maximum calls which may be made on the State for relief purposes, there are a number of other questions which such an estimate does not presume to touch. The necessity for remissions of the Land Revenue, for advances to the cultivators, and similar demands with a view to preventing rural disorganisation, are questions for local experience and the actual events of the season to decide. It would be unprofitable for me to enter on them.

Nor will any amount of liberality and wisdom in dealing with a famine avert a great deal of intense suffering. In my separate accounts of Midnapur, Nadiyá, and the 24 Parganás (*post*, pp. 142-147, 177-186, 169-177) I have given rather fuller details of the Famine of 1866 than in the other Districts. These

* Annals of Rural Bengal, p. 37, Fifth Edition.

three Districts lie close to Calcutta; were under the public gaze from the first; and had very fair facilities for transport. Yet the sufferings of the people were intense. Not so intense, however, as they would have been if the Government had done nothing. Under Native Rule, when the crops failed, the people died. No human efforts could contend with the vindictiveness of the gods. According to the Bengali proverb, which I myself heard in 1866, "It is watering the top of a tree whose roots are cut;" *Gora katiya agay jal dhala.* But a civilised Government can do much to mitigate the suffering which it cannot altogether avert. It is to a large degree a question of knowledge. In 1770, with an expenditure of £9000, one-third of the whole population perished. In 1866, with an expenditure of £254,689, from one-half to three-quarters of a million people died of hunger or of diseases incident to semi-starvation. It remains to be seen what record of human suffering, but also of well-directed human effort, next year will leave behind it. Private benevolence and organised relief are even more important than State charity, and as a matter of fact, Government only contributed £143,788 *net* to the £254,689 spent in 1866. But Government must take the lead, and it is only with the official aspects of the case that I have here to deal.*

* As regards the Famine of 1769–70, I have given an abstract of the Official Records and Government Consultations and Proceedings in Appendix B to my "Annals of Rural Bengal," page 399 *et sequitur.* In Appendix A to that work, page 379, *et sequitur*, I have reproduced Warren Hastings' Official Report on the state of Bengal in 1772, two years after the famine. For a more general account see page 19 to 63, chap. ii, of my "Annals of Rural Bengal." For a brief and popular account of the Famines of 1837-38 and 1860-61, see pages 51 and 52 of that work. In my "Orissa," vol. ii. pp. 174 to 199, I have gone into the fundamental aspects of famine, and the permanent costliness to Government of an uncontrolled and unhusbanded water supply.

TABULATED STATEMENT

SHOWING

FAMINE RATES, FAMINE WARNINGS, TOTAL POPULATION, WITH ESTIMATES OF THE AGRICULTURISTS AND LABOURERS IN EACH OF THE FORTY DISTRICTS.

I. Name of District.	II. Total Population.	III. Agricultural Population.	IV. Labourers and poorer Craftsmen.	V. Total of Agricultural population and Labourers.	VI. Highest price of Rice per maund as retd. by District Officers. Famine of 1866.*	VII. Famine Prices as retd. by District Officers. Rice per maund.†	VIII. Famine Warnings as estimated by District Officers. Rice per maund in January.‡
PATNA DIVISION.							
Patná	1,559,638	598,794	540,009	1,138,803	Rs. 5–8	Rs. 3–8	Rs. 1–9
Gayá	1,949,750	749,061	704,631	1,453,692	,, 6–10	,, 5–8 *a*(?)	,, 2–10
Sháhábád	1,723,974	769,515	475,194	1,244,709	,, 4–7	,, 3–5 *b*	,, 2–13*c*
Sáran	2,063,860	1,235,391	311,493	1,546,884	,, 4–8	,, 3–0	,, 2–13
Tirhut	4,384,706	2,830,254	689,037	3,519,291	,, 5–6 *d*	,, 3–5 to 5 *e*	,, 2–3 to 2–8
Champáran	1,440,815	1,019,646	266,055	1,285,701	Information not received.		
Total	13,122,743	7,202,661	2,986,419	10,189,080	Av. Rs. 5–4½	Av. Rs. 3–14	Av. Rs. 2–7
BHAGALPUR DIVISION.							
Bhágalpur	1,826,290	980,322	505,926	1,486,248	Rs. 5–0	Rs. 4–0	Rs. 2–8
Purniah	1,714,795	830,034	581,844	1,411,878	,, 4–7	,, 5–0 *f*	loss of 6–13th of crops.
Monghir	1,812,986	792,564	593,883	1,386,447	,, 5–0	,, 3–5 to 4–0	Rs. 2–8
Santál Parganás—							
Rájmahal	... ...	... ...	... ...	... ...	5–11 to 6–10	2–13 to 4–0	,, 2–13
Deogarh	1,259,287	614,919	360,114	975,033	Rs. 6–0	Rs. 3–5 *g*	,, 2–10
Nayá Dumká	... ...	... ...	... ...	... ...	,, 6–8	,, 4	,, 2–10
Total	6,613,358	3,217,839	2,041,767	5,259,606	Av. Rs. 5–8	Av. Rs. 3–14	Av. Rs. 2–9

RAJSHAHI DIVISION.

Rájsháhí	1,310,729	715,749	276,465	992,214	Rs. 5-0	Rs. 5	Rs. 2-8
Rangpur	2,149,972	1,637,838	281,235	1,919,673	,, 5-0	,, 5-0 *h*	...
Murshidabad	1,353,626	532,248	432,009	964,257	,, 6-10	,, 4-0	Rs. 2-8
Pabna	1,211,594	602,652	269,142	871,794	,, 3-14	,, 4-0	Not given.
Bogra	689,467	507,294	68,820	576,114	,, 4-0	,, 4	Rs. 3
Dinajpur	1,501,924	1,083,705	1247,323	1,331,028	,, 4-1	,, 4	Not given.
Maldah	676,426	305,382	186,060	491,442	,, 4-0	Rs. 4-0	Ditto.
Total	8,893,738	5,384,868	1,761,654	7,146,522	Av. Rs. 4-10	Av. Rs. 4-4	Av. Rs. 2-10

KUCH BEHAR DIVISION.

Jalpaiguri	418,665	246,720	33,654	280,374	No famine.	Rs. 4 to 5	No chance of famine.
Goalpara	407,714	307,959	56,385	364,344	No famine.	,, 5 to 7-8	Rs. 5-0
Kuch Behar }	532,565	}	... ...	... ...	Rs. 6, but no famine.	,, 5 to 6	,, 3-0
Garo Hills }	80,000	no	population	details	No famine.		no criterion.
Darjiling	94,712	57,861	36,066	93,927	Rs. 5	Price of grain Rs. 3-5 to 5 *i*	Rs. 2 *j*
Total	1,533,656	612,540 *k*	126,105 *k*	1738,645 *k*	Av. Rs. 5-8	Av. Rs. 5-1	Av. Rs. 3-5

* Except when specially mentioned in the text, I take these prices from the special returns prepared for me by the District Officers, not from the Famine Commissioners' report. † *i.e.* The point at which the District Officer thinks that relief operations become necessary. ‡ *i.e.* The rates which, if reached shortly after the *aman* harvest of December, would justify apprehension of famine before the next *aus* harvest of the succeeding August. *a.* The District Officer gave a rough estimate of 4 times ordinary rates, and returned ordinary rates to me in 1871 at Rs. 1-6. If the ordinary rate be taken at Rs. 1, as other Collectors estimate it, famine prices in Gaya would be Rs. 4. *b.* Relief operations become urgent at Rs. 5. *c.* From Collectors' special report. *d.* Average of four localities in August. In one place prices had touched Rs. 8. *e.* "8 to 12 seers per rupee." *f.* Rs. 5 imminent famine; Rs. 6-10 absolute famine. *g.* Paddy at 25 seers per rupee—rice at 12 seses. *h.* "Justifies intervention of Government." *i.* Rs. 3-5 on the *tarai*; Rs. 5 in the hills. Certain hill-men estimated famine rates at Rs. 8, but the District Officer thinks that long before this price was reached, the hill-men would have migrated. *j.* Rice "rapidly rising above Rs. 1-5." *k.* Exclusive of Kuch Behar Proper and Gáro Hills.

I. Name of District.	II. Total Population.	III. Agricultural Population.	IV. Labourers and poorer Craftsmen.	V. Total of Agricultural Population and Labourers.	VI. Highest price of Rice per maund as retd. by District Officers. Famine of 1866.* ‡	VII. Famine Prices as retd. by District Officers. Rice per maund.†	VIII. Famine Warnings as estimated by District Officers. Rice per maund in January.‡
CHOTA NAGPUR DIVISION.							
Hazaribagh	771,875	416,505	191,775	608,280	Rs. 5–0	Not given.	Not given.
Lohardaga	1,237,123	686,013	226,977	912,990	,, 3–12	Rs. 4–8	Rs. 2–8 *a*
Singhbhúm	415,023	219,015	114,294	333,309	,, 3–10	Not given.	,, 2–8
Manbhúm	995,570	506,391	257,238	763,629	,, 8–0	Not given.	,, 2–10
Tributary States	405,980	256,560	85,926	342,486	Not given.	Not given.	Not given.
Total	3,825,571	2,084,484	876,210	2,960,694	Av. Rs. 5–1	Rs. 4–8	Av. Rs. 2–8
BARDWAN DIVISION.							
Bardwán	2,034,745	974,223	604,839	1,579,062	Rs. 5–5	Rs. 5–0	Rs. 2–8
Bírbhúm	696,945	354,450	179,325	533,775	,, 5–0	,, 3–5	Not given.
Bánkura	526,772	227,853	177,726	405,579	,, 7–4	,, 4–0 *b*	Rs. 2–10 *c*
Húgli and Howrah	1,488,556	565,659	479,349	1,045,008	,, 5–2	,, 4–0	,, 2–13 *d*
Midnapur	2,540,963	1,395,654	631,302	2,026,956	,, 8–0	,, 4–0	,, 2–8
Total	7,287,981	3,517,839	2,072,541	5,590,380	Av. Rs. 6–2	Av. Rs. 4–1	Av. Rs. 2–10

PRESIDENCY DIVISION.

24 Parganas	1,951,137 *e*	915,639	562,908	1,478,547	Rs. 5-11	Rs. 3-12	Rs. 2-8
Nadiya	1,812,795	716,172	514,113	1,230,285	,, 5-0	,, 3-10	,, 2-40
Jessor	2,075,021	1,245,147	373,791	1,618,938	,, 4-0	,, 5-0	Not given.
Total	5,838,953	2,876,958	1,450,812	4,327,770	Av. Rs. 4-14	Av. Rs. 4-2	Av. Rs. 2-6

ORISSA DIVISION.

Balasor	770,232	404,985	136,662	541,647	Rs. 13-0	Rs. 3-3 *f*	Rs. 2-7
Cattack	1,494,784	618,372	386,118	1,004,490	,, 10-0	,, 3-13	,, 2-0
Purí	769,674	371,436	184,467	555,903	,, 7-4	Not available.	
Total	3,034,690	1,394,793	707,247	2,102,040	Av. Rs. 10-1	Av. Rs. 3-8	Av. Rs. 2-3

a. After the Indian corn harvest, in subdivision Palámau, a famine warning would be Rs. 3-8; but this subdivision does not depend upon its rice crop, and rice rates do not form an adequate criterion. *b. i.e.,* Price of rice in May 1866; but see also para. 11 of the District Narrative in the Famine Commissioners' Report, vol. i. p. 328. *c.* The Collector gives Rs. 3, but also mentions double ordinary rates and gives Rs. 1-4 a maund as that rate. The price in January 1866, as returned by the Famine Commissioners, was 15 seers per rupee, or Rs. 2-10 per maund, and I have taken this figure. *d.* 14 3-16th seers per rupee, the lowest of the three rates, reported by the Famine Commissioners in January 1866. *e.* Exclusive of Calcutta, the suburbs and the shipping. *f.* The rate returned by the Collector at which the non-cultivating labouring classes cannot afford to buy rice.

N.B.—The price rates returned from Kuch Behar Division have but little significance. The lowland parts have hitherto been exempt from famine, and no materials exist for a well-founded forecast of famine rates. In the hill tracts the price of rice is no criterion, as the aborigines live on other food, and in time of famine would migrate or fall back upon edible roots. As they seldom buy or sell rice, market rates can scarcely be said to exist for this commodity among the hill-rates.

DISTRICT ACCOUNTS.

DISTRICT ACCOUNTS.

PATNA DISTRICT.

Famine Prices, 1866 and 1869.—The maximum prices of grain in Patná during the famine of 1866 are reported by the Collector as follow:—Shelled rice, Rs. 5-8; and unhusked rice, Rs. 3-8 per maund. In 1868-69, the District suffered from drought, and local prices were as follow:—Rice, Rs. 3-4; paddy, Rs. 1-12; and Indian corn, Rs. 2-4 a maund. In January 1870, the Collector reported to me that local prices had not returned to the ordinary rates which prevailed before the famine year. The rates in ordinary years are returned for paddy from 14 annas to Re. 1-4 per maund; and for rice, Re. 1-8 a maund.

Famine Warnings.—In 1870, the Collector reported that prices may be considered to have reached famine rates, that is to say, the point at which relief operations become necessary, when rice sells at Rs. 3-8, paddy at Rs. 2-4, Indian corn at Rs. 2-4, and wheat at Rs. 3 a maund, as the mass of the people could scarcely afford to purchase food at these rates. Long-continued drought during the rainy season, resulting in an almost total loss of the winter rice harvest, when coupled with the absence of rain at the time of sowing the *rabi* or spring crop, should be considered a distinct warning of famine. If there has been a previous succession of good harvests, with an accumulation of rice stores in the District, a single bad winter rice crop would not produce absolute famine, provided it has been preceded by a good *aus* or autumn harvest, as Indian corn and *janirah* are largely consumed by the people. The scarcity of 1869 following so soon after the famine of 1866, made the distress greater than what would be ordinarily caused by the failure of a single winter rice crop. The *rabi*, or spring crop of 1869, however, was a fair one, and averted absolute famine. Had this crop failed, distress would have been very severe. A serious rise in the price of grain, soon after the gathering of the *aman* or winter rice harvest, is another warning of famine. The Collector states that if unhusked rice were selling at Rs. 1-5 to Rs. 1-9 a maund in January or February, it should be looked upon as a warning of famine later in the year. The Collector reports that Patná District mainly depends upon the *aman* or winter rice crop for its food supply. The *aus* or autumn crop could not compensate for an almost total loss of the *aman* harvest.

MEANS OF TRANSIT.—Ample facilities exist for the importation of grain in seasons of scarcity, by means of the Ganges, the line of railway, and the various imperial and local roads passing through the District. The Collector, however, reported to me in 1870 that a road from Bakhtiárpur railway station to Behar is a great want, and ought to be supplied. As a means of protection against famines, which in Patná District are caused by excessive drought, and not by floods or rainfall, the Collector suggested that the construction of tanks and reservoirs would be very beneficial.

OUT-TURN OF CROPS.—The Collector states that no statistics exists with regard either to the total area under cultivation, or the comparative acreage under the principal crops. A fair outturn from a *bigha* of land paying a rent of Rs. 1-8 a *bigha*, would be about five maunds of paddy, value Rs. 4. The class of land produces no second crop. For the superior descriptions of land, paying a rent of Rs. 3 a *bigha*, the Collector reports that a fair medium out-turn would be eight maunds of paddy per *bigha*, value Rs. 6-6; besides a second crop of pulses, worth about Rs. 2; total value of crop, Rs. 8-6 per *bigha*.

AGRICULTURAL POPULATION.—The Collector has furnished me with no particulars regarding the proportion of agriculturists to labourers. But the Census Report of 1872 (pp. cxxvii., cxxviii.) gives the total "Agricultural and Pastoral Castes" (Hindus) of the Patná District at 451,197, including males, females, and children; but exclusive of Musalmáns who live by agriculture, and of the aboriginal and semi-aboriginal castes partly living by cultivation. But by analysing the details of population arranged according to occupation at pp. clxix., clxx., I find that the total male adults of class iv., *i.e.*, persons engaged in agriculture or with animals, is 212,529. Allowing two other souls as an average of females and children connected with each male adult, the total population living by agriculture or in connection with animals, amounts to 637,587. Deducting 12,931 male adults for the "excepted classes" explained at a foregoing page, *i.e.*, persons possessing estates or otherwise well off, a balance remains of 199,598 males under class iv.; or allowing two other persons to each male adult, a total population of 598,794 souls living by husbandry or employed in connection with animals, or tenure-holders belonging to classes who are often people in a small way. This is the *gross* agricultural population. The total number of male adult "cultivators" as returned by the Census is 191,651, or, taking the average of two souls to each male adult as family and children, a total population of 574,953. The male adults directly employed in cultivation form about one-fourth of the total males in the District; and the total number of males, females, and children living by cultivation (as estimated by my analysis of class iv.) amounts to 598,794, or more than one-third of the total population of the District (1,559,638).

LABOURING POPULATION.—The Census Report, in its statement of castes and nationalities (pp. cxxvi.–cxxix.), returns the labouring classes, below the rank of artisans, of the Patná District as follow:—

1. Aboriginal tribes	429
2. Semi-Hinduised aboriginals	215,149
3. Personal servant castes	137,839
4. Weaver castes	23,558
5. Labouring castes	28,778
6. Boating and fishing castes	23,752
7. Musician and vagabond castes	1,357
8. Unclassified, Vaishnavs, &c.	15,194
Total ...	446,056

Turning to the statement of occupations (pp. clxv.–clxxix.), I find the following numbers under the six classes. I only take those who may fairly be considered in the rank of labouring men:—

			ADULT MALES.
Class I.	(*Govt. employ*)	Piyádás	9
Class II.	(*Professionals*)	Musicians	279
Class III. *Service*		Personal servants, ...	27,085
		Sweepers	474
		Water-carriers ...	132
		Unspecified	83

Class V. *Conveyance of goods.*	Cartmen ...	...	552
	Bullock-drivers	...	3,498
	Palki-bearers	...	2,841
	Boatmen ...	...	5,502
Class VI. *Poorer sorts of craftsmen.*	Lime-burners	...	218
	Diggers ...	...	2,671
	Basket-makers	...	987
	Cotton-spinners	...	13,800
	Shoe-makers	...	2,063
	Cotton-carders	...	1,268
	Bird-catchers	...	146
Class VII. *Miscellaneous.*	Beggars ...	...	4,886
	Labourers ...	...	103,578
	Unemployed	...	9,931
	Total	...	180,003

The total population of the District is 1,559,638. Taken by castes, therefore, there are 446,056 persons belonging to labouring classes, or more than a fourth of the total population. According to occupation there are 180,003 male adults, who may fairly be considered in the rank of labouring men, or 540,009 males, females, and children, comprising over one-third of the total population.

The foregoing calculations give therefore the net results :—

1.	Total population	1,559,638
2.	Agriculturists (Hindus), according to caste statement	451,197
3.	Agriculturists (total), according to occupation statement	598,794
4.	Labourers (Hindus and aborigines), according to caste	446,056
5.	Labourers (total), according to occupation ...	540,009
6.	Total of Hindu agriculturists and labourers, according to caste statement	897,253
7.	Total of all agriculturists and labourers, according to occupation statement	1,138,803

N.B.—It should be remembered that the occupation totals are obtained by multiplying the *male adults* by three, and that this proportion is perhaps a little too high.

GAYA DISTRICT.

FAMINE PRICES.—The maximum price of rice in Gayá District during the famine of 1866 is returned to me by the Collector at six seers for the rupee, or Rs. 6-10 a maund, and of paddy 12 seers for the rupee, or Rs. 3-5 a maund. Subsequent harvests were good, especially the winter crop of 1870, and the Collector in February 1871, reported that prices had returned to their normal rates before the famine year; the rates for common rice were returned to me in February 1871 at Rs. 1-6, and paddy at 12 annas a maund.

Famine rates in Gayá may be considered to have been reached when rice sells at four times its ordinary price. The staple crop of the District is rice, and when this sells at from six to seven seers for the rupee, prices have reached a point at which the Collector reported to me that relief operations became necessary. At these rates, the landless classes cannot support themselves out of the hire which they ordinarily receive for daily labour; while the cultivators whose crops have failed, would find it difficult to obtain loans from the *Zamindars* or the *Mahajans*, unless they were well provided with a stock of cattle.

FAMINE WARNINGS.—The Collector reported to me that the absence of heavy showers during June and July should be regarded as a warning of approaching famine. Another indication is, the price of rice at the time of the *aman* or winter harvest. If at that time, or shortly after the gathering in of this crop, the price of rice is as high as Rs. 2-10 a maund, or 15 seers for the rupee, it should be looked upon as a sign of famine later in the year. The Collector's report states that no *aus* or autumn rice is grown in Gayá; the people, therefore, have to depend entirely upon the *aman* or winter harvest, with the *rabi* crops.

MEANS OF TRANSIT.—The only means at the disposal of the District for importing rice in times of famine, is the Patná branch road, but the Collector stated that the carriage is expensive, and that the imported grain comes to as high prices as those prevailing in the interior of the District. He reported that the *Zamindars* can always retain large stores of grain in hand to meet emergencies, and the District produces sufficient grain in ordinary years to feed its own population. The only remedial measures which the Collector suggested to me as necessary during famines, are Government relief works in the form of opening out roads or canals. Of these two measures the latter would probably be the more productive, as irrigation would tend to prevent the occurrence, and certainly to mitigate the effects of future famines.

CULTIVATED AREA; OUT-TURN OF CROPS.—No information exists as to the total cultivated area, as the records of the Revenue Survey were burned during the mutiny. The Collector, however, reported to me in 1871, the proportion of land under food-crops to be as follows:—Rice 65 per cent. of the total cultivated area; wheat 5 per cent.; gram 5 per cent.; peas 7 per cent.; barley 10 per cent.; *musuri* 8 per cent. First quality land he estimated to yield 10 maunds of paddy per *bigha*, and from inferior lands, six maunds of paddy, worth in 1871 about 14 annas a maund; besides a second crop of pulse worth from 12 annas to Re. 1 a maund. The Collector stated that very little land was let out in Gayá District at a money rental. He reported that the usual arrangement in regard to rice lands was for the landlord to take half the produce of the fields in lieu of rents.

AGRICULTURISTS.—The Collector gives me no statistics regarding the proportion of the agricultural and labouring population. But the Census Report of 1872 (pp. cxxvii., cxxviii.) returns the total "Agricultural and Pastoral Castes" (Hindus) of the Gayá District at 481,693, including males, females, and children; but exclusive of the Musalmáns who live by cultivation, and aboriginal or semi-aboriginal castes, partly living by agriculture. But by analysing the details of population, arranged according to occupation at pp. clxix., clxx., I find that the total male adults of class iv., *i.e.*, persons engaged in agriculture or with animals, is 264,306. Allowing two other individuals as an average for females and children connected with each male adult, the total population living by agriculture or by tending animals, amounts to 792,918. Deducting 14,619 male adults for the "excepted classes," explained at a foregoing page (*i.e.*, persons possessing estates or otherwise well off), a balance remains of 249,687 males under class iv.; or allowing two other persons to each male adult, a total population of 749,061, living by actual husbandry, or employed in connection with animals, or tenure-holders belonging to the classes who are generally people in a small way. This may be taken as the *gross* agricultural population. The total number of male adult "cultivators," as returned by the Census, is 236,723, or, allowing an average of two souls to each male adult as family and children, a *net* population of 710,169 actual cultivators.

LABOURING POPULATION.—The Census Report in its statement of Castes and Nationalities (pp. cxxvi.-cxxix.) returns the labouring classes, below the rank of artisans, of the Gayá District, as follow. Some of these figures have been corrected from the District Census compilation subsequently drawn up by Mr C. F. Magrath. They were erroneously entered in the Census Report:—

1. Aboriginal tribes	5,882
2. Semi-Hinduised aboriginals	403,243
3. Personal servant castes	167,479
4. Weaver castes	14,347
5. Labouring castes	31,257
6. Boating and fishing castes	12,694
7. Musician and vagabond castes	1,246
8. Unclassified, Vaishnavs, &c....	11,158
Total ...	647,333

Turning to the statement of occupations (pp. clxv.-clxxix.), I find the following numbers under the several classes. I only take those who may fairly be considered in the rank of labouring men:—

		MALE ADULTS.
Class II. (*Professionals*)	Musicians	713
Class III. *Service.*	Personal servants ...	5,288
	Sweepers	303
	Water-carriers ...	23
	Unspecified	27,150
Class V. *Conveyance of goods.*	Cartmen	912
	Palki-bearers	2,011
	Boatmen	285
Class VI. *Poorer craftsmen.*	Lime-burners	228
	Diggers	1,853
	Basket-makers ...	1,839
	Cotton-spinners ...	19,827
	Shoe-makers	3,545
	Cotton-carders ...	1,354
	Bird-catchers	108

Class VII. *Miscellaneous.*	Beggars	5,585
	Labourers	153,533
	Unemployed	10,320
	Total ...	234,877

The total population of Gayá District is 1,949,750. Taken by castes, 647,333 persons are returned as belonging to labouring classes, or about one-third of the total population. According to occupation, there are 234,877 male adults, or 704,631 males, females, and children, being about three-eighths of the total population.

The foregoing calculation yields the following results :—

1. Total population	1,949,750
2. Agriculturists according to castes (Hindus)	481,693
3. Gross agricultural population according to occupation	749,061
4. Labouring population according to castes (Hindus, aborigines and semi-aborigines)	647,333
5. Labouring population acccording to occupation (all)	704,631
6. Total agriculturists and labourers according to caste statement (Hindus, aborigines, &c.)	1,129,026
7. Total agriculturists and labourers according to occupation statement	1,453,692

N.B.—It must be remembered that the total number of agriculturists and labourers, according to occupation, is obtained by multiplying the number of male adults by three.

SHAHABAD DISTRICT.

FAMINE PRICES.—The maximum price of rice in Sháhábád during the famine of 1866-67 was reported to me by the Collector at Rs. 4-7 a maund, or 9 seers for the rupee, and of paddy, Rs. 2-10 a maund, or 15 seers for the rupee. There was also a severe scarcity in 1868-69. On both these occasions Government stepped in with relief measures, which were undertaken with great watchfulness and care. The Collector in a report to me, dated June 1871, states that by a timely attention to the commencement of relief works, the distribution of food in charity (which has a most demoralising effect on the people) may be generally avoided. Professional beggars, and the labouring poor who are reduced in strength, might be formed into separate squads and put to light work proportionate to their strength. On this point the District Engineer, in a report on the scarcity of 1869, wrote as follows :—

Under these circumstances I have formed what the people themselves call a *Kangali* or beggar squad, in which I have drafted all those who are in bad case, and where they are made to work according to their ability to do so. By this means the remaining working parties or able-bodied, are left susceptive of the checks and measurement of work, by which alone a fair out-turn can be obtained for the money expended. The usefulness of the *Kangali* or beggar squads was most marked. To them is to be attributed the absence of that demoralising aid, gratuitous relief, which for a few days was forced on the Magistrate of Baxar owing to the number of beggars who at one time flocked into the station. These people were drafted into the *Kangali* or beggar squads, where they had to do light work proportionate to their strength, and were paid daily; but even the little restraint that this occasioned was irksome to the professional beggars, and most of them soon returned to their accustomed haunts and scattered throughout the District."

Famine Warnings.—The Collector in 1871 reported to me that prices had returned to what were considered their ordinary rates before the famine. Judging from the results of 1866 and 1869, he stated that if rice were selling at the rate of Rs. 3-5 a maund or 12 seers for the rupee soon after the crop had been harvested, or in January or February, it would be necessary to commence relief operations. He reports that this rate was reached in January 1869. Sháhábád District mainly depends upon the *aman* or winter harvest, and a fair yield of this would enable the people to tide over any deficiency or failure of the *rabi* or spring crop.

Means of Transit.—The means of communication at the disposal of the District for the purpose of importing grain in times of scarcity, are reported exceedingly deficient, especially during the rains when such importations are most needed. As an illustration of this, the Collector states that in 1869, grain was selling at 30 per cent. higher rates in the southern and interior parts of the District than in the part near the line of railway. On this point the District Engineer reported as follows :—"In looking back on the circumstances connected with the late distress, it is impossible to doubt that the large importations of grain into the District warded off the famine that was impending, and the inhabitants, rich and poor, bespeak blessing on the railway. But the railway was not all that was needed. The grain had to be distributed throughout the District, and the imperfect condition of the local roads rendered this a task of the utmost difficulty. During the rains when the importations were greatest, the Sasseram and Arrah road, which is the principal line in the District, was crowded with traffic; and it was painful to witness long strings of carts, half a hundred in a line, cutting their way through a foot deep of puddle. The road is *kacha* (*i.e.*, unmetalled), and with the traffic that was on it, mud and water, do what we might, would produce puddle; so that in the interior of the District particularly towards the south, grain was selling at from 30 to 40 per cent. higher rates than at the railway station."

CULTIVATED AREA; OUT-TURN OF CROPS, &c.—The Collector in June 1871 returned the cultivated area at 1,763,200 acres, or 2755 square miles, out of a total area of 4403 square miles. A fair average out-turn from a *bigha* of good rice land paying a rent of Rs. 3 a *bigha*, is estimated by the same authority at 5 maunds of paddy valued Rs. 5, and 4 maunds of a second crop valued at Rs. 6; total Rs. 11. From a *bigha* of inferior land at half the above rent, a fair out-turn would be 2½ maunds of paddy valued Rs. 2-8, and 2½ maunds of second crop, valued at Rs. 3-12; total Rs. 6-4.

PRICE CURRENTS.—The prices in 1862 were as follow:—

Coarse rice in ordinary use ...	30 seers per rupee.
Pulses	50 " "
Wheat	22 " "

The prices obtaining in the year 1866 were as follow:—

Coarse rice in ordinary use, ...	9 seers per rupee.
Pulses	10 " "
Wheat, cheapest sort	9 " "

The Collector reported to me that the Railway works in the District has created a class of labourers many of whom had wholly withdrawn themselves from agricultural pursuits. A large number of such labourers are now employed in the Soane irrigation works. Labourers not possessing lands of their own, but employed to till the lands of others, are called Bhuinhars in the District. Women are largely employed in the fields.

Agricultural Population.—I have obtained no statistics from the Collector under this head. But the Census Report of 1872 (pp. cxxvii., cxxviii.) gives the total "Agricultural and Pastoral Castes" (Hindus) of the Sháhábád District at 441,621, including males, females, and children, and exclusive of the Musalmáns who live by cultivation, and of the aboriginal or semi-aboriginal tribes, partly living by agriculture. But by analysing the details of population arranged according to occupation, at pp. clxix., clxx., I find that the total male adults of class iv., *i.e.*, persons engaged in agriculture or with animals, is 270,959. Allowing two other individuals as an average for the females and children connected with each male adult, the total population living by agriculture or by tending animals amount to 812,877. Deducting 14,454 male adults for the "excepted classes," explained at a foregoing page, *i.e.*, persons possessing estates or otherwise well off, a balance remains of 256,505 males under class iv., or allowing two other persons to each male adult, a total population of 769,515 souls living by actual husbandry, or employed in connection with animals, or tenure holders belonging to the classes who are generally people in a small way. This represents the *gross* agricultural population. The total number of male adult "cultivators," as returned by the Census, is 246,805, or taking the average of two souls to each male adult as family and children, a *net* cultivating population of 740,415.

Labouring Population.—The Census Report in its Statement of Castes and Nationalities (pp. cxxvi.-cxxix.) returns the labouring classes,* below the rank of artisans, of the Sháhábád District as follows:—

1. Aboriginal tribes	13,245
2. Semi-Hinduised aborigines	230,368
3. Personal servant castes	85,384
4. Weaver castes	12,153
5. Labouring castes	22,193
6. Boating and fishing castes	20,398
7. Musician and vagabond castes	218
8. Unclassified, Vaishnavs, &c.	11,731
Total ...	395,690

* The figures have been corrected from the District Census Statements subsequently compiled by C. F. Magrath, Esq., now in charge of Census.

Turning to the Statement of Occupations (pp. clxv.–clxxix.), I find the following numbers under their respective classes. I only take those who may fairly be considered in the rank of labouring men :—

		MALE ADULTS.
Class I. (*Government employ*)	Piyádás	5
Class II. (*Professionals*)	Musicians	195
Class III. *Service.*	Personal servants	2,780
	Sweepers	484
	Water-carriers	54
	Unspecified	15,130
Class V. *Conveyance of goods.*	Cartmen	903
	Palki-bearers	1,905
	Boatmen	1,563
Class VI. *Poorer craftsmen.*	Lime-burners	92
	Diggers	273
	Basket-makers	1,369
	Cotton-spinners	13,034
	Shoe-makers	4,677
	Cotton-carders	1,777
	Bird-catchers	403
Class VII. *Miscellaneous.*	Beggars	5,860
	Labourers	99,445
	Unemployed	8,449
	Total	158,398

The total population of the Sháhábád District is 1,723,974. Taken by castes, therefore, there are 395,690 persons belonging to the labouring classes, or above one-fifth of the total population. According to occupation there are 158,398 male adults, or 475,194 males, females, and children, being more than one-fourth of the total population.

The foregoing calculations yield the following results :—

1. Total population	1,723,974
2. Agriculturists according to castes (Hindus)...	441,621
3. Agricultural population according to occupation (total)	769,515
4. Labouring population according to castes (Hindus, aborigines and semi-aborigines)	395,690
5. Labouring population according to occupation (total)	475,194

6. Hindu agricultural and labouring population according to caste statement 837,312
7. Total gross agricultural population and labourers, according to occupation statement ... 1,244,709

N.B.—It must be remembered that the total of agriculturists and labouring population, according to occupation, is obtained by multiplying the number of male adults by three.

SARAN DISTRICT.

FAMINE PRICES.—The maximum price of paddy and rice during the famine of 1866-67 is reported to me by the Collector to have been Rs. 3 and 4-8 per standard maund. The point at which relief for the able-bodied poor should commence, is, in his opinion, reached when the price of grain rises 50 per cent. over the average rates, especially if the market at the same time shows an upward tendency. The Collector in his report to me, January 1871, states that it would then become necessary to distribute food in charity. But if food does not rise more than 50 per cent., he thinks the able-bodied would be capable of supporting themselves and dependants.

The Collector would not recommend the opening of gratuitous relief operations until staples, which ordinarily sell at 30 seers per rupee, or Rs. 1-5 a maund, should rise to 13 or 14 seers for the rupee, or from Rs. 2-13, to Rs. 3. But he would advocate the opening of relief works as soon as it is ascertained that the ordinary labourer or small cultivator has become unable to earn sufficient to keep his family in health; and this point is in his opinion reached when the purchasing power of wages has decreased to one-half.

FAMINE WARNINGS.—The Collector considers the first warning of a famine is the loss of two out of the three crops, especially if these should happen to be the winter and spring crops, the rain crops being comparatively insignificant. Great pressure may be predicted, if not actual famine from April to September, after a total failure of the winter crops, along with a probable failure of the spring crop, the prospects of which are always pretty well ascertained by the middle of January. The scarcity would, however, be sensibly relieved by the rain crops if they proved favourable. In making these calculations, the Collector assumed a general failure of crops in the adjoining Districts. A merely local failure of the crops in Sáran would not produce famine, although it might cause distress among the agriculturists.

MEANS OF TRANSIT.—Sáran is well intersected with unmetalled roads which are passable even in the rainy season, and the Collector thought there would be no difficulty in distributing imported grain throughout the District.

AREA UNDER TILLAGE, AND OUT-TURN OF CROPS.—The Collector returns the approximate acreage under the principal crops as follows:—Rice 475,000 acres; wheat 275,000, other edible grain 322,320; probable total area under cultivation 1,252,820 acres. Fifteen maunds of paddy are considered a first-class yield for a *bigha* of rice-land, and from 9 to 11 maunds of paddy a good average yield. Land yielding 9 or 10 maunds to the *bigha* is considered inferior; soils yielding less than 5 or 6 maunds are reported as scarcely worth cultivating. The price of paddy in ordinary years is stated at 30 standard seers for the rupee. It is not general to take a second crop from rice-lands, but in some rice-lands *khesari* and gram are sown by the cultivators before the rice is cut and without any ploughing. Such a second crop gives a small out-turn averaging 3 or 4 maunds *per bigha.* But the best rice-lands are never cropped twice. The Collector reports to me that 25 *bighas* of land yield a comfortable maintenance for a husbandman's family, and renders him better off than a shopkeeper with a clear profit of 8 Rs. a month. The prices of the principal grains in 1871 were returned by the Collector as follow:—

Cleaned rice	12 to 16	seers per rupee.
Do. do. coarse quality	20 to 25	"
Unshelled rice, best quality	20 to 25	"
Do. do. coarse quality	35 to 40	"
Maize	40	"
Barley	30	"
Wheat	18	"

AGRICULTURAL POPULATION.—The Collector does not furnish any statistics regarding the proportion of agricultural and labouring population. The Census Report of 1872 (pp. cxxvii., cxxviii.) gives the total "Agricultural and Pastoral Castes" (Hindus) in the Sáran District at 508,687, as corrected by the subsequent District Census Statement, including males, females, and children, and exclusive of the Musalmáns who live by cultivation, and of aboriginal or semi-aboriginal castes who partly employ themselves in agriculture. But by analysing the details of population arranged according to occupation at pages clxix., clxx., I find that the total male adults of class iv., *i.e.*, persons engaged in agriculture or with animals, is 427,810. Allowing two other souls as an average of females and children connected with each male adult, the total population living by agriculture or by connection with animals amounts to 1,283,430. Deducting 16,013 male adults for the "excepted classes" explained at a foregoing page, *i.e.*, persons possessing estates or otherwise well off, a balance remains of 411,797 males under class iv.; or estimating two other persons to each male adult, a total population of 1,235,391, living by actual husbandry, or employed in connection with animals, or tenure-holders belonging to the classes who are often people in a small way. This represents the *gross* agricultural population. The total number of male adults "cultivators," as returned by the Census, is 408,333, or adding two other persons to each male adult for women and children, a total of 1,224,999. The male adults employed in cultivation form a little less than half of the total males in the District; and the net cultivating population, males, females, and children (as estimated by my analysis of class iv.), amounts to 1,224,999, or three-fifths of the total population of the District, namely, 2,063,860.

LABOURING POPULATION.—The Census Report in its statement of Castes and Nationalities (pp. cxxvi.–cxxix.) returns the labouring classes, below artisans, of the Sáran District as follow, the figures being corrected from the subsequent District Census Statements:—

1. Aboriginal tribes	7,796
2. Semi-Hinduised aboriginals	213,468
3. Personal servant castes	86,225
4. Weaver castes	10,460
5. Labouring castes	67,273
6. Boating and fishing castes	38,352
7. Musician and vagabond castes	47
8. Unclassified, Vaishnavs, &c.	29,456
Total ...	453,077

Turning to the statement of occupations, I find the following

numbers under the several classes. I only take those who may be fairly considered in the rank of labouring men :—

		MALE ADULTS.
Class II. (*Professionals*)	Musicians	343
Class III. *Service.*	Personal servants ...	2,977
	Sweepers	377
	Water-carriers	2
	Unspecified	16,377
Class V. *Conveyance of goods.*	Cartmen	1,783
	Palki-bearers	2,096
	Boatmen	4,828
Class VI. *Poorer craftsmen.*	Lime-burners	181
	Diggers	10
	Basket-makers ...	1,991
	Cotton-spinners ...	13,329
	Shoe-makers	1,624
	Cotton-carders ...	2,456
	Bird-catchers	57
Class VII. *Miscellaneous.*	Beggars	3,722
	Labourers	47,469
	Unemployed	4,209
	Total ...	103,831

The total population of the Sáran District is 2,063,860. Taken by castes, therefore, there are 453,077 persons belonging to labouring classes, or more than one-fifth of the total population. According to occupation, there are 103,831 male adults, or 311,493 males, females, and children, being less than one-sixth of the total population. As a rule, the Occupation Statement should show a larger result than the Caste Statements, for it includes Musalmáns as well as Hindus. In this District, however, either the *chamars* are agriculturists, or the Census Report fails us altogether. Thus the Caste Statement shows 94,844 *chamars*, while the Occupation Statement shows only 1624 shoe-makers and 1360 tanners and dealers in hides. The same sort of discrepancy is found with regard to the Personal Servant Castes.

The foregoing calculations yield the following results :—

1. Total population 2,063,860
2. Agriculturists according to caste statement (Hindus) 508,687

3. Gross agricultural population according to occupation statement 1,235,391
4. Labouring population according to caste statement (Hindus, aborigines, and semi-aborigines) 453,077
5. Labouring population according to occupation (total) 311,493
6. Total agriculturists and labourers according to caste statement (Hindus, &c.) ... 961,764
7. Total agriculturists and labourers according to occupation statement (all) 1,546,884

N.B.—It must be remembered that the total of agriculturists and labourers is according to occupation, and is obtained by multiplying the number of male adults by three.

TIRHUT DISTRICT.

Famine Prices.—The maximum price of rice during the famine of 1866 was Rs. 8 a maund, or 5 seers to the rupee; and for paddy Rs. 4-7 a maund, or 9 seers for the rupee. The following statement is compiled from a return of the price of food grains at the principal market towns in Tirhut, dated 27th August 1866, when the famine was at its height. (1.) Muzaffarpur, the headquarters station.—Cheapest description of rice, Rs. 5 a maund; cheapest sort of pulses in ordinary use, Rs. 4-3 a maund; wheat, Rs. 4-7 a maund; *janirah*, Rs. 3-10 a maund. (2.) Darbhángá town.—Common rice, Rs. 6-2½ a maund; common pulses, Rs. 7-4 a maund; wheat, Rs. 6-10½ a maund; *janirah* and *joar*, Rs. 5-5 a maund. (3.) Hájípur.—Common rice, Rs. 4-7 a maund; common pulses, Rs. 3-13 a maund; wheat, Rs. 4-5 a maund. (4.) Sitámári.—Common rice, Rs. 5-15 a maund; common pulses, Rs. 5-15 a maund; wheat, Rs. 5-5 a maund, and *janirah* and *joar*, Rs. 3-6 a maund. These rates are reported to me as considerably more than double the average prices at the same season of other years. There was another very severe scarcity in 1869, but prices did not reach the excessive rates which they did in 1866. The Collector thinks that local prices in 1871 may be said to have generally returned to what were considered their ordinary level before the famine of 1866.

FAMINE WARNINGS.—The Collector states that it is not easy to lay down any particular rates at which relief operations would become necessary, as prices taken by themselves do not afford a sufficient criterion. If rice were selling at Rs. 2-3 a maund or 18 seers for the rupee after the harvesting of the winter crops, in January or February, and the spring crop also proved a failure, there would (later in the year) be more suffering and want among the labouring classes than there would be even if the price of rice had been higher than Rs. 2-3 a maund in January, provided that the spring crop was a fair one. But in the anticipation of a failure of the spring crops as well as the winter harvest, from drought (which is the only cause of famine in Tirhut), a rate of 16 to 18 seers per rupee in January should be considered as indicative of severe pressure from May to September. These rates, although not perhaps indicating actual famine, might render it advisable for the State to begin relief works (particularly in the southern part of the District, which depends largely on the spring harvest). A rate of from 14 to 16 seers per rupee in January or February would probably render relief operations expedient on a large scale. The rate in August and September in such a year, would probably reach 8 to 12 seers per rupee.

MEANS OF TRANSIT.—Tirhut being usually an exporting District, importations even in a bad year cannot (in the opinion of the Collector) be looked for on any sufficient scale, although good means of communication exist by road and river. Even in the famine year of 1866 exportation went on from the District.

CULTIVATED AREA; OUT-TURN OF CROPS.—The Collector in his report to me, dated March 1871, returned the approximate area of the District at 6114 square miles or 3,913,221 acres, of which he estimated about three-fourths might be calculated as under tillage, and the remaining one-fourth occupied by village sites, mango groves, rivers, roads, waste lands, &c. A fair out-turn of paddy from the local *bigha* (35,156 square feet) of good land is returned at 20 maunds, and from a local *bigha* of inferior land at from 7 to 10 maunds, valued at Rs. 14 and Rs. 7 or Rs. 8 respectively. Reduced to the standard *bigha* of 14,400 square feet, a fair out-turn for good lands would be about $8\frac{1}{4}$ maunds, and for inferior lands from $2\frac{3}{4}$ to $4\frac{1}{8}$ maunds. But the Collector mentions that the yield of land in the different parts of the District varies considerably. He gives the above as an average calculation. A holding of more than 70 *bighas* is considered large; one below ten *bighas* is reckoned below the adequate size. A fair-sized holding would be 25 *bighas.* In the south of the District, where the lands are generally high and yield two crops in the year, a holding of forty *bighas* would be considered large. The majority of the husbandmen are here reported to be small cultivators with less than 5 *bighas*, and a man with 15 *bighas* would be considered comfortably off. A cultivator of 15 *bighas*, having no other resource, is not so well off as a respectable retail shopkeeper, except in the south of the District. A salary of Rs. 8 a month in money would not enable a man to live so well as by a holding of 15 *bighas*. The wages of a coolie vary from 1½ to 3 annas a day. The agricultural labourers, however, do not receive their wages in cash, but are paid in grain. The Collector reports the daily rates of wages in kind to be from 1½ seers to 2 seers besides some bread, and occasionally a little quantity of *satu* (parched grain reduced to meal) at noon. The following were returned in 1871 as the ordinary prices of food-grains :—

Best rice in ordinary use	...	...	22	seers per rupee.
Common do.	...	...	24	"
Barley do.	...	...	30	"
Best paddy do.	...	...	35	"
Common paddy do.	...	...	38	"
Indian corn do.	...	...	32	"

Wheat is not in common use; it is sold at 20 seers for a rupee.

Agricultural Population.—The Census Report of 1872 (pp. cxxvii., cxxviii.) gives the total Agricultural and Pastoral Castes (Hindus) of the Tirhut District at 964,296, including males, females, and children, and exclusive of the Musalmáns who live by cultivation, and of the aboriginal or semi-aboriginal tribes partly living by agriculture. But by analysing the details of population arranged according to occupation at pp. clxix., clxx., I find that the total male adults of class iv., *i.e.*, persons engaged in agriculture or in tending animals, is 973,299. Allowing two other persons as an average of females and children connected with each male adult, the total population living by agriculture or in connection with animals amounts to 2,919,897. Deducting 29,881 male adults for the "excepted classes," *i.e.*, as explained at a foregoing page, persons possessing estates or otherwise well off, a balance remains of 943,418 males under class iv., or allowing two other persons to each male adult, a total population of 2,830,254 souls living by actual husbandry or employed in connection with animals, or tenure-holders belonging to classes who are generally people in a small way. This number represents the *gross* agricultural population. The total number of male adult "cultivators" as returned by the Census is 938,132, or taking the average of two individuals to each male adult for women and children, a *net* cultivating population of 2,814,396. This average is here probably too high.

The male adult "cultivators" form about three-sevenths of the total males in the District; and allowing two other persons to each male adult, the total of males, females, and children living by cultivation would amount to 2,814,396, or about two-thirds of the total population of the District (4,384,706).

LABOURING POPULATION.—The Census Report in its statement of Castes and Nationalities returns the labouring classes, as corrected by the subsequent District Census Compilation, below the rank of artisans, of the District of Tirhut, as follows :—

1. Aborigines	2,247
2. Semi-Hinduised aborigines	615,929
3. Personal servant castes	320,147
4. Weaver castes	161,970
5. Labouring castes	87,054
6. Boating and fishing castes	219,509
7. Beggars and vagabond castes	3,488
Total ...	1,410,344

Turning to the statement of occupations, I find the following numbers under their respective classes. I only take those who may fairly be considered in the rank of labouring men.

		MALE ADULTS.
Class II. (*Professional*)	Musicians	247
Class III. *Service.*	Personal servants ...	4,849
	Sweepers	808
	Water-carriers	76
	Unspecified	30
Class V. *Conveyance of goods.*	Cartmen	2,586
	Palki-bearers	5,585
	Boat-men	1,970

Class VI. *Poorer craftsmen.*	Lime-burners	159
	Diggers	117
	Basket-makers	2,807
	Cotton-spinners ...	22,504
	Shoe-makers	2,688
	Cotton-carders	3,484
	Bird-catchers	80
Class VII. *Miscellaneous.*	Beggars	7,843
	Labourers	152,350
	Unemployed	21,496
	Total ...	229,679

The total population of the Tirhut District is 4,384,706. Taken by castes, therefore, there are 1,410,344 persons belonging to labouring classes, or about one-third of the total population. According to occupation, there are 229,679 male adults, or 689,037 males, females, and children, being something above one-seventh of the total population.

The foregoing calculation yields the following results:—

1. Total population 4,384,706
2. Agriculturists according to caste statement (Hindus) 964,296
3. Agriculturists according to occupation statement (total) 2,830,254
4. Labouring population according to caste statement (Hindus, aborigines, and semi-aborigines) 1,410,344
5. Labouring population according to occupation (total) 689,037
6. Total agriculturists and labourers according to caste statement (Hindus, aborigines, &c.) 2,374,640
7. Total agriculturists and labourers according to occupation statement (all) 3,519,291

N.B.—It must be remembered that the total of agriculturists and labourers, according to occupation statement, is obtained by multiplying the number of male adults by three. The great difference in results yielded by the Caste and Occupation Statements (both for the agricultural and the labouring population), probably arises from the circumstance that a large population of the Semi-Hinduised Aborigines, such as the *Dosadhs*, are husbandmen and labourers.

CHAMPARAN DISTRICT.

Agricultural Population.—The Collector of the District in his report gives no information either as to the famine of 1866, or what prices may be considered as famine rates, or the proportion of the agricultural to the labouring population. On this latter point the Census Report of 1872 (pp. cxxvii., cxxviii.) returns the total "Agricultural and Pastoral" Castes (Hindus) of Champáran at 320,468, including males, females, and children, but exclusive of Muhammadans, who follow agriculture, and aboriginal or semi-aboriginal tribes partly living by cultivation. But by analysing the details of population arranged according to occupation, pp. clxix., clxx., I find that the total male adults of class iv., *i.e.*, persons engaged in agriculture or in tending animals, is 342,822. Allowing two other persons as an average of females and children connected with each male adult, the total population living by agriculture, or in connection with animals, amounts to 1,028,466. Deducting 2940 male adults for the "excepted classes," explained at a foregoing page, *i.e.*, persons possessing estates or otherwise well off, a balance remains of 339,882 males under class iv., or allowing two other persons to each male adult, a total population of 1,019,646 souls living by actual husbandry or employed in connection with animals, or tenure-holders belonging to classes who are often people in a small way. This may be taken as the *gross* agricultural population. The total number of male adult "cultivators" as returned by the Census is 337,484, or taking the average of two persons to each male adult as family and children, a total *net* agricultural population of 1,012,452.

The male adults employed in cultivation form about three-sevenths of the total males in the District; and the total number of males, females, and children living by cultivation (as obtained by allowing two other persons to each male adult) amounts to 1,012,452, or about five-sevenths of the total population of the District (1,440,815).

Labouring Population.—The Census Report in its statement of Castes and Nationalities (pp. cxxvi.-cxxix.) returns the labouring classes, below the rank of artisans, of the Champáran District, as follow. The figures have been corrected from the subsequent District Census Statements:—

1.	Aborigines	31,203
2.	Semi-Hinduised aborigines	221,462
3.	Personal servant castes	58,914
4.	Weaver castes	28,234
5.	Labouring castes	36,068
6.	Boating and fishing castes	62,757
7.	Beggar and vagabond castes	32
8.	Unspecified, Vaishnavs, &c.	16,851
	Total	455,521

Turning to the statement of occupations (pp. clxv., clxxix.), I find the following numbers under their respective classes. I only take those who may fairly be considered in the rank of labouring men. The figures have been checked from the subsequent District Census Statement, compiled by Mr C. F. Magrath:—

		MALE ADULTS.
Class II. (*Professionals*)	Musicians	85
Class III. *Service.*	Personal servants	1,874
	Sweepers	160
	Unspecified	9,426
Class V. *Conveyance of goods.*	Cartmen	1,317
	Palki-bearers	694
	Boatmen	928
Class VI. *Poorer craftsmen.*	Lime-burners	102
	Diggers	27
	Cotton-spinners	2,811
	Shoe-makers	494
	Basket-makers	1,133
	Cotton-carders	575
	Bird-catchers	32
Class VII.	Beggars	2,659
	Labourers	63,118
	Unemployed	3,250
	Total	88,685

The total population of the District is 1,440,815. Taken by castes, therefore, there are 455,521 persons belonging to labouring classes, or about one-third of the total population. According to occupation, there are 88,685 male adults, or allowing two other persons to each adult as family, a total of 266,055 males, females, and children, being about one-fifth of the total population. The difference probably arises from many of the Semi-Hinduised Castes being engaged as husbandmen and not as labourers.

The foregoing calculations yield the following results :—

1. Total population	1,440,815
2. Agriculturists according to caste statement (Hindus)	320,468
3. Agriculturists according to occupation statement	1,019,646
4. Labouring population according to caste statement (Hindus, aborigines, &c.) ...	455,521
5. Labouring population total according to occupation	266,055
6. Total (Hindu) agriculturists and labourers according to caste statement	775,989
7. Total of all agriculturists and labourers according to occupation statement ...	1,285,701

N.B.—It must be remembered that the total of agriculturists and labourers, according to occupation, is obtained by multiplying the number of male adults by three.

BHAGALPUR DIVISION.

BHAGALPUR DISTRICT.

Famine Prices. — The maximum price of rice in Bhágalpur District during the famine of 1866-67, was returned by the Collector at 8 seers per rupee, and of paddy 16 seers. The Collector in his report to me in 1870 stated that local prices had then returned to their ordinary rates before the famine. Famine rates may be considered to have been reached in this District when rice has risen to ten seers per rupee, or perhaps even before that. The Collector would take the condition of Midnapur District in 1866 as a guide; the two Districts being fairly capable of comparison, about the same size, and possessing a very similar climate and general geological character. A large portion of the further limits of both are covered with jungle, and inhabited by aboriginal or primitive tribes. He thinks that the external communication of both Districts is on a par, the Ganges running through Bhágalpur, and the Húglí by Midnapur; 300 miles of railway connect Bhágalpur with Calcutta and the North-West; 70 miles of road connect Midnapur with Calcutta, and it has also the advantage of a canal and a seaboard.

In 1866 (he continues) the Collector of Midnapur considered that famine point would not be reached till rice was selling at eight seers per rupee or Rs. 5 per maund; on its reaching that point, he owned that he had waited too long. With this experience, the Collector of Bhágalpur does not think it would be safe fixing famine point beyond the time when rice sells for 10 seers per rupee.

Famine Warnings.—A rainfall of sparse quantity and of short duration should be taken as warning of famine, especially if there is no rain in October or November. A great rise in prices after the *aman* or winter harvest would be looked upon by the

Collector as a serious warning, and the loss of even half this crop as a very urgent warning. In the case of rice reaching 16 seers per rupee or Rs. 2-8 per maund in January or February, a famine should be expected later in the year. The *aus* or autumn crop of Bhágalpur is very small, and could not make up for an almost total loss of the *aman* or winter rice, nor avert actual famine for the year.

MEANS OF TRANSIT.—The railway, rivers, and roads in the north of the District afford easy intercommunication, and thus supply the first necessity for encountering a famine. The same cannot, however, be said regarding the Bánká subdivision in the south. Here there are no rivers or canals, and the roads are not good. In the rains it is of difficult access, and if famine prevailed at that period of the year, the throwing of grain into it would be a matter of great difficulty, expense, and time; and the want of communication would be severely felt. Bánká, however, has one protection against famine which does not apply to places richer and better situated. Rice does not form the staple food of the poor in Bánká, and a rice famine therefore touches them but little. The moisture of the hilly jungles is sufficient to protect the hardy *mahua* and *kasundi* from drought, and to these the very poor classes of Bánká are more accustomed than to rice.

OUT-TURN OF CROPS.—The Collector states that he can furnish no returns relative to the proportion of cultivated and uncultivated areas, but so far as he can learn a fair out-turn from a *bigha* of land paying a rent of Rs. 1-8 would be five maunds of paddy, and from a *bigha* paying Rs. 3 as rent, the out-turn would be about twice as much. The price of paddy not only varies every year, but differs according to the time of year, locality, and quality. The Collector is of opinion, however, that the price of ordinary paddy at Bhágalpur town ranges from 1½ maunds per rupee at the cheapest time of the year just after the harvest, to 35 seers per rupee at the dearest time. In addition to rice, a second crop of pulses or oil seeds is raised on *aus* lands in the cold weather, the out-turn from which, in the opinion of the Collector, would make up the total value of the produce from a *bigha* of land paying a rental of Rs. 1-8, to about Rs. 6 or Rs. 7; and from a *bigha* of land paying Rs. 3 as rent to about Rs. 12 or 13.

AGRICULTURAL POPULATION.—I have obtained no information on this head from the Collector, but the Census Report (pp. cxxvii., cxxviii.), gives the total "Agricultural and Pastoral Castes" (Hindus) of the District at 456,278, including males, females, and children; but excluding Musalmáns who follow agriculture, and the aboriginal and semi-aboriginal tribes living by cultivation. The figures have been corrected from the subsequent District Census Statements. But by analysing the details of population arranged according to occupation at pp. clxix., clxx., I find that the total male adults of class iv., *i.e.*, persons engaged in agriculture or in tending animals, is 331,925. Allowing two other persons as an average of females and children connected with each male adult, the total population living by agriculture or in connection with animals amounts to 995,775. Deducting 5151 male adults for the "excepted classes," as explained in a foregoing page, *i.e.*, persons possessing estates or otherwise well-off, a balance remains of 326,774 males under class iv., or allowing two other persons to each male adult, a total population of 980,322 souls living by actual husbandry or employed in connection with animals, or tenure-holders belonging to classes who are often people in a small way. This may be taken as the *gross* agricultural population. The total number of male adult "cultivators" as returned by the Census is 321,897, or taking the average of two persons to each male adult for women and children, a *net* cultivating population of 965,691.

The male adults employed in cultivation form above one-third of the total males in the District; and the total number of males, females, and children (as obtained by allowing two other persons to each male adult) amounts to 965,691, or more than half of the total population of the District (1,826,290).

Labouring Population.—The Census Report in its statement of Castes and Nationalities (pp. cxxvi.–cxxix.), returns the labouring classes, below the rank of artisans, of the Bhágalpur District, as follow. The figures have been corrected from the subsequent District Census Statements:—

1. Aborigines	31,186
2. Semi-Hinduised aboriginals	317,943
3. Personal servant castes	170,119
4. Weaver castes	98,906
5. Labouring castes	31,557
6. Boating and fishing castes	118,557
7. Beggar and vagabond castes	2,748
8. Unspecified, Vaishnavs, &c.	17,197
Total ...	788,213

Turning to the statement of occupation (pp. clxv.–clxxix.), I find the following numbers under their respective classes. I only take those who may fairly be considered in the rank of labouring men.

Class	Occupation	MALE ADULTS.
Class II. (*Professionals*)	Musicians	165
Class III. *Service.*	Personal servants ...	1,284
	Sweepers	88
	Unspecified	26,564
Class V. *Conveyance of goods.*	Cartmen	1,723
	Palki-bearers ...	1,478
	Boatmen	2,901
Class VI. *Poorer craftsmen.*	Lime-burners ...	110
	Diggers	446
	Cotton-spinners ...	10,581
	Shoe-makers ...	1,212
	Basket-makers ...	1,312
	Cotton-carders ...	1,762
	Bird-catchers ...	33
Class VII. *Miscellaneous.*	Beggars	2,416
	Labourers	111,436
	Unemployed ...	5,131
	Total ...	168,642

The total population of the Bhágalpur District is 1,826,290. Taken by castes, therefore, there are 788,213 persons belonging to labouring classes, or three-sevenths of the total population. According to occupation, there are 168,642 male adults, or allowing two other persons to each, 505,926 males, females, and children, being about three-tenths of the total population. The discrepancies between the results obtained from the Caste and Occupation Statements probably arise from the fact, that a large proportion of the aboriginal and semi-aboriginal tribes (who are here entered as labourers) are in reality cultivators. But they form the lowest class of husbandmen, and on the approach of famine abandon their fields to seek hired labour, and are thus thrown on the labouring population.

The foregoing calculations yield the following net results:—

1. Total population 1,826,290
2. Agriculturists according to caste statement (Hindus) 456,278

3. Agriculturists according to occupation (all) ... 980,322
4. Labouring population according to caste statement (Hindus, aborigines, &c.) ... 788,213
5. Labouring population according to occupation (all) 505,926
6. Total agriculturists and labourers according to caste statement (Hindus, aborigines, &c.) 1,244,491
7. Total agriculturists and labourers according to occupation (all) 1,486,248

N.B.—It must be remembered that the total of agricultural and labouring population, according to occupation, is obtained by multiplying the number of male adults by three.

PURNIAH DISTRICT.

Famine Prices.—The Collector reported to me in August 1872, that during the famine of 1866 the maximum prices of food grains were for the best quality of rice Rs. 5 a maund, and for common rice Rs. 4-7-1 a maund. He also stated that prices had not then returned to the rates which prevailed before the famine of 1866, but remained at about the rates of 1865. He did not consider that famine rates were reached in Purniah in 1866. A Relief Committee was formed, but found nothing to do. The high prices of 1866 did not last long, as the next winter rice crop put matters to rights. The highest price which could be borne by the people without absolute famine would be rice at Rs. 6-10-8 a maund. The peculiarity of Purniah is that the rainfall differs a good deal in different parts of the District; hence the crop varies according to the locality, and universal loss is unknown.

Famine Warnings.—The Collector would regard a loss of crops in more than 6 *thanas* or police circles out of a total of 13 *thanas*, or a serious rise after the reaping of the *aman* or winter crop, as likely to cause scarcity amounting to famine. In the opinion of the Collector, rice selling at Rs. 5 a maund in January would be a warning of imminent famine. The people depend mainly upon the *aman* crop, and even in the event of the entire loss of the *aus* harvest, the winter crop would be sufficient to support the population.

MEANS OF TRANSIT.—The District possesses ample means for importation in time of famine. It has numerous navigable rivers, with a branch of the Great Trunk Road, and various inter-District roads which run through the interior.

CULTIVATED AREA; OUT-TURN OF CROPS.—The Statistical Returns compiled for 1870-71 estimate a total cultivated area in Purniah District of 2,315,910 acres, or 3618.61 square miles; 285,440 acres, or 446 square miles uncultivated, but capable of being brought under tillage; and 571,029 acres, or 892.23 square miles uncultivable. Of the cultivated area, by far the greater quantity is under rice. The area under food crops in 1870-71 was returned as follows:—Rice, 1,736,932 acres; wheat, 46,318 acres; other food grains, 46,318 acres; vegetables, 69,477 acres; total, 1,899,045 acres, out of a total cultivated area of 2,315,910 acres. An average yield from ordinary land is returned at 4½ maunds of paddy per *bigha*, worth from 8 to 12 annas a maund; a second crop of other grain, such as *janirah* or *kulthi*, estimated at two to three maunds per *bigha*, worth from 8 to 12 annas a maund; or of mustard seed, which yields from two to three maunds, value from Rs. 1-8 to Rs. 2, with a maund. The Collector states that a fair gross return from a *bigha* of ordinary land paying a rent of Re. 1, would be a little more than 6½ maunds of produce, value about Rs. 7-12.

AGRICULTURAL POPULATION.—The Census Report of 1872 (p. cxxvii.) returns the total "Agricultural and Pastoral Castes" (Hindus) of the Purniah District at 247,993, including males, females, and children, but exclusive of Muhammadans who follow agriculture, and aboriginal or semi-aboriginal tribes partly living by cultivation. But by analysing the details of population arranged according to occupation (pp. clxix., clxx.), I find that the total male adults of class iv., *i.e.*, persons engaged in agriculture or in tending animals, is 278,863. Allowing two other persons as an average of females and children connected with each male adult, the total population living by agriculture or in connection with animals amounts to 836,589. Deducting 2185 male adults for the "excepted classes" explained at a foregoing page, *i.e.*, persons possessing estates or otherwise well off, a balance remains of 276,678 males under class iv., or allowing two other persons to each male adult, a total population of 880,034 souls living by actual husbandry or employed in connection with animals, or tenure-holders belonging to classes who are often people in a small way. This may be taken as *gross* agricultural population. The total number of male adult "cultivators" as returned by the Census is 271,938, or taking the average of two persons to each male adult as family and children, a *net* cultivating population of 815,814.

The male adults employed in actual cultivation form about one-third of the total males in the District; and the total number of males, females, and children living by cultivation, as obtained by allowing two other persons to each male adult, amounts to 815,814, or about half of the total population of the District (1,714,795).

LABOURING POPULATION.—The Census Report in its statement of Castes and Nationalities (pp. cxxvi.-cxxix.) returns the labouring classes, below the rank of artisans, of the Purniah District, as follow. I have corrected the figures from the subsequent District Census Statements by Mr C. F. Magrath :—

1.	Aborigines	19,794
2.	Semi-Hinduised aboriginals	237,534
3.	Personal servant castes	83,482
4.	Weaver castes	61,974
5.	Labouring castes	8,999
6.	Boating and fishing castes	87,364
7.	Beggar and vagabond castes	2,643
8.	Unspecified, Vaishnavs, &c.	42,994
	Total ...	544,784

Turning to the Statement of Occupations (pp. clxv.-clxxix.), I find the following numbers under their respective classes. I only take those who may fairly be considered in the rank of labouring men :—

		MALE ADULTS.
Class II. (*Professionals*)	Musicians	268
Class III. *Service.*	Personal servants ...	2,255
	Water-carriers	42
	Sweepers	228
	Unspecified	30,744
Class V. *Conveyance of goods.*	Cartmen	2,367
	Palki-bearers	1,195
	Boatmen	2,164

Class VI. *Poorer craftsmen.*	Basket-makers ...	1,112
	Lime-burners	155
	Diggers	299
	Cotton-spinners ...	8,695
	Cotton-carders ...	599
	Bird-catchers	78
Class VII. *Miscellaneous.*	Beggars	3,056
	Labourers	132,596
	Unemployed	8,095
	Total ...	193,948

The total population of District is 1,714,795. Taken by castes, therefore, there are 544,784 persons belonging to the labouring classes, or about one-third of the total population. According to occupation, there are 193,948 male adults, or 581,844 males, females, and children, being just over one-third of the total population.

The foregoing calculations yield the following results. The discrepancy between the figures obtained for the agriculturists from the Caste and Occupation Statements, probably arises from the fact that a large proportion of the aboriginal and semi-aboriginal tribes (who are here entered as labourers) are in reality cultivators. But they form the lowest class of husbandmen, and on the approach of famine abandon their fields to seek hired labour, and are thus thrown on the labouring population :—

1. Total population	1,714,795
2. Agriculturists according to castes (Hindus)	247,993
3. Agriculturists according to occupation (all)	830,034
4. Labouring population according to castes (Hindus, aborigines, and semi-aborigines)	544,784
5. Labouring population according to occupation (all)	581,844
6. Total agriculturists and labourers according to caste statement (Hindus, &c.) ...	792,777
7. Total agriculturists and labourers according to occupation statement (all)	1,411,878

N.B.—It must be remembered that the total of agriculturists and labourers according to occupation is obtained by multiplying the number of male adults by three.

MONGHIR DISTRICT.

FAMINE PRICES.—The highest rates for paddy and rice during the famine of 1866 is reported by the Collector to have been 13 and 8 seers per rupee respectively. The Collector in a return to me in 1871 states that the rates had then recovered from the effect of that famine, but that as the tendency of prices is upwards, it is improbable that there will be a recurrence of the old low rates. He thinks that famine prices are reached when rice sells at from 10 to 12 seers per rupee.

FAMINE WARNINGS.—The partial failure of the *aus* crop, followed by the total failure of the *aman* or winter crop, would be sufficient to cause famine. If rice were selling shortly after harvest in January and February at 16 seers for the rupee, or Rs. 2-8 per maund, it would be looked upon as a warning of approaching famine. The District depends on its rice crops, and the Collector reported that no other crops could compensate for their failure.

MEANS OF TRANSIT.—Two lines of the East Indian Railway run through Monghir, and these, together with good river communication, afford sufficient security against the isolation of the District in times of distress.

REMEDIAL MEASURES.—The only remedial measure suggested by the Collector in case of famine, is the prompt importation and storing of grain.

OUT-TURN OF CROPS.—The average yield of a *bigha* of paddy-land in Monghir District, paying a rental of Rs. 1-8, is reported to me by the Collector to be from 3 to 4 maunds, valued at from Rs. 2-8 to Rs. 3-8; and of superior lands paying Rs. 3 as rent, from 6 to 9 maunds of paddy, valued at from Rs. 5 to Rs. 7-8. Rice-lands in this District do not generally yield a second crop.

AGRICULTURAL POPULATION.—The Collector of the District in his Report gives no information as to the proportion of agriculturists as compared with labouring population of the District, but the Census Report of 1872 (pp. cxxvii., cxxviii.) returns the total "Agricultural and Pastoral Castes" (Hindus) of the Monghir District at 339,093, including males, females, and children, but exclusive of the Muhammadans who follow agriculture, and aboriginal or semi-aboriginal tribes partly living by cultivation. But by analysing the details of population arranged according to occupation (pp. clxix., clxx.), I find that the total male adults of class iv., *i.e.*, persons engaged in agriculture or in tending animals, is 277,541. Allowing two other persons as an average of females and children connected with each male adult, the total population living by agriculture or in connection with animals amounts to 832,623. Deducting 13,353 male adults for the "excepted classes" explained at a foregoing page, *i.e.*, persons possessing estates or otherwise well off, a balance remains of 264,188 males under class iv.; or allowing two other persons to each male adult, a total population of 792,564 souls living by actual husbandry or employed in connection with animals, or tenure-holders belonging to classes who are often people in a small way. This may be taken as the *gross* agricultural population. The total number of male adult "cultivators" as returned by the Census is 255,295, or taking the average of two persons to each male adult as family and children, a *net* cultivating population of 765,885.

The male adults employed in cultivation form about three-tenths of the total males in the District; and the total number of males, females, and children living by cultivation (as estimated by allowing two other persons to each male adult) amounts to 765,885, or about two-fifths of the total population of the District (1,812,986).

Labouring Population.—The Census Report in its statement of Castes and Nationalities (pp. cxxvi.–cxxix.) returns the labouring classes, below the rank of artisans, of the Monghir District, as follows. The figures have been corrected from the subsequent District Census Statements by Mr C. F. Magrath :

1. Aborigines	21,672
2. Semi-Hinduised aboriginals	327,017
3. Personal servant castes	197,019
4. Weaver castes	87,824
5. Labouring castes	30,181
6. Boating and fishing castes	57,834
7. Beggar and vagabond castes	5,476
8. Unspecified, Vaishnavs, &c.	14,419
Total	741,442

Turning to the Statement of Occupations (pp. clxvi.–clxxix.), I find the following numbers under their respective classes. I only take those who may fairly be considered in the rank of labouring men :—

		MALE ADULTS.
Class II. (*Professionals*)	Musicians	432
Class III. *Service.*	Personal servants ...	2,346
	Sweepers	420
	Water-carriers ...	240
	Unspecified ...	21,461
Class IV. *Conveyance of goods.*	Cartmen	908
	Palki-bearers ...	2,485
	Boatmen	8,962
Class VI. *Poorer craftsmen.*	Lime-burners ...	63
	Diggers	1,131
	Basket-makers ...	1,496
	Cotton-spinners ...	13,417
	Shoe-makers ...	3,598
	Cotton-carders ...	1,430
Class VII. *Miscellaneous.*	Beggars	3,253
	Labourers	128,672
	Unemployed ...	7,647
	Total ...	197,961

The total population of the District is 1,812,986. Taken by castes, therefore, there are 741,442 persons belonging to labouring classes, or about two-fifths of the total population. According to occupation there are 197,961 male adults, or allowing two other persons to each, a total of 593,883 males, females, and children, being about one-third of the total population. The discrepancy in the labouring population according to Caste Statement and that according to Occupation arises from the fact that a large number of aboriginal and semi-aboriginal tribes live wholly or partly by agriculture. But they are so improvident and poor, and so many of them turn labourers on the approach of a scarcity, that I have thought it best to reckon them as such.

The foregoing calculations yield the following results :—

1. Total population	1,812,986
2. Agriculturists according to caste statement (Hindus)	339,093

3. Agriculturists according to occupation (all) 792,564
4. Labouring population according to caste statement (Hindus, aborigines, &c.) ... 741,442
5. Labouring population according to occupation 593,883
6. Total agriculturists and labourers according to caste statement (Hindus, aborigines, &c.) 1,080,535
7. Total agriculturists and labourers according to occupation (all) 1,386,447

N.B.—It must be remembered that the totals of agricultural and labouring population according to occupation are obtained by multiplying the *male adults* by three.

SANTAL PARGANAS.

RAJMAHAL SUB-DISTRICT.

Famine Prices.—The Assistant Commissioner reported to me in 1870, that during the famine of 1865-66 and 1867 the maximum price of rice was 6 or 7 seers per rupee, but that the local prices had then (1870) returned to what were considered as their ordinary rates before the famine.

Famine Warnings.—The fact of the price of rice rising to 10 or 14 seers, of paddy to 20 or 25 seers, of Indian corn to 20 seers, and *kulthi* to 12 seers per rupee, would tend to indicate that prices were verging on famine rates, and relief operations would become necessary.

A labourer's daily income may be reckoned at 3 annas; his household generally consists of himself, his wife, and three children, to feed whom 4 seers of rice, ½ seer of *dal*, and 2 *chataks* of salt, &c., daily, would be required, costing at the above rates 6 annas per diem, or about double the amount of his average daily earning. Should these rates be reached in January or February, shortly after the *aman* or winter rice harvest, the Assistant Commissioner would consider it a warning of famine later in the year.

Out-turn of Crops.—In this District the *aus* rice harvest is very small, and Indian corn takes its place. The District chiefly depends on the *aman* crops. In the event of the almost total failure of this harvest, the Indian corn and *aus* crops would enable the people to live for a few months, but not throughout the year, without actual famine. The Assistant Commissioner reported in 1870 that the means at the disposal of the District were sufficient to avert the extremity of famine by importation from other parts; the only part liable to isolation was the Daminikoh, but railway feeders were then under construction and nearly finished, which would place this tract out of danger. The Assistant Commissioner added that he considered the importation of grain, with construction of roads and other public works, would afford adequate remedial measures during a famine in that division of Rájmahal.

The total area of the District is 1200 square miles, of which 800 square miles, or 3-4ths, are stated to be under cultivation, 200 square miles cultivable, and 200 square miles incapable of cultivation. No estimate of the comparative average under the principal crops can be given, as no data exist on the subject. For *aus* land 8 annas to Re. 1 is the usual rent paid for a standard *bigha* in Khás Rájmahal division. In the *Pákur* sub-division 10 and 16 maunds of paddy are considered a fair yield per *bigha* for land paying rent at Rs. 1-8 and Rs. 3 respectively. The average value of the paddy from the former land is Rs. 6-10-8, and from the latter Rs. 10-10-8. In addition to the rice crops, a second crop of pulses or oil seeds may be raised, which would yield 3 maunds per *bigha*, the price of which, at a rough estimate, may be Rs. 1-8 per maund.

DEOGARH SUB-DISTRICT.

Famine Prices.—The Assistant Commissioner in his report to me, dated March 1871, states that the highest price of paddy during the famine of 1866 was 12 seers, and of rice 6½ seers the rupee. The local prices had then (1871), with the exception of one or two articles, fallen to the same rates which prevailed before the famine. When paddy sells at 25 seers, and *janirah* at 15 seers, the people are reduced to distress, and unable to purchase or obtain credit from their *mahajans*. It then in the opinion of the Assistant Commissioner becomes necessary to give Government relief.

FAMINE WARNINGS.—If there be no rain or a very scanty supply in the months of June or July, it may be considered as a warning of famine. The following rates, if reached in January or February, are considered as a warning of famine later in the year. Paddy 30 seers per rupee, rice 15 seers per rupee, Indian corn 20 seers per rupee. *Aus* paddy is not generally grown in this District, the staple crops being *aman* rice, Indian corn, and other high-land crops. Were the Indian corn and other early crops to fail, the *aman* crop, if not a bad one, would be sufficient; but if the *aman* were to fail, the Indian corn and other crops would not enable the people to live through the year without famine. The people are almost entirely dependant on the *aman* crops.

MEANS OF TRANSIT.—The Chord Line of the East Indian Railway was opened on the 1st January 1871, and the Assistant Commissioner states that there is now no risk of isolation in case of a famine. Imported grain can be sent to any portion of the District from the railway stations.

OUT-TURN OF CROPS.—A standard *bigha*, paying rent of Rs. 1-8, will yield, on an average, from 6 to 8 maunds of paddy, and a *bigha* paying Rs. 3, from 10 to 12 maunds of paddy, of an average value of Re. 1 per maund. No second crop of paddy is taken from the same land in one year. But in lands sown with *shathia* paddy, which is reaped in August, a second crop of wheat or oats is sometimes obtained. A fair return from a *bigha* of rice-land, renting at Rs. 1-8, is reported by the Assistant Commissioner to be Rs. 8 per year. If the land be sown with *shathia* rice, 6 maunds of paddy would be an average yield worth Rs. 6, besides 3 maunds of wheat or oats worth Rs. 6; total yield, 9 maunds of produce valued at Rs. 12. Land renting at Rs. 3 per *bigha* should yield 12 maunds of paddy worth Rs. 12 per year.

AGRICULTURAL POPULATION.—The District may be said to be entirely agricultural, the proportion of non-agriculturists being very small. More precise details are not available.

NAYA DUMKA SUB-DISTRICT.

FAMINE PRICES.—The maximum price of paddy and rice during the famine of 1866-67 was Rs. 6-8 and Rs. 4 per maund respectively.

FAMINE WARNINGS. — The Assistant Commissioner in his report, dated May 1871, states that judging from the experience of former years, he should say that the Government would have to institute relief works if the price of rice rose to 10 seers and *janirah* to 15 seers per rupee. He would also consider it a warning of impending famine if there was a partial failure of the Indian corn and a serious failure of the rice crops. In 1868-69 there was cause of alarm, but the Indian corn and rice proved abundant in 1869-70, and fears were relieved. The Assistant Commissioner reported, that if the rate of rice rose to 15 seers and *janirah* to 20 seers per rupee in January, the markets should be carefully watched; export of *janirah* to Hazaribagh, which at times is very extensive, is apt to upset all calculation. It is believed that the people at the end of 1868 were seriously alarmed and stopped the exportation of *janirah;* and so averted distress.

COMMUNICATIONS.—The imperial road leading to Suri on the south and to Bhágalpur on the north, forms the main artery of the District, but its usefulness is very greatly impaired for want of a few bridges, which have long been proposed, but the construction of which has been delayed.

MEANS OF TRANSIT.—Measures suggested in case of return of famine.—The Assistant Commissioner is not aware of any measures which could be resorted to, except gratuitous relief and employment on public works.

CULTIVATED AREA, AND OUT-TURN OF CROPS.—The total area of this division is 1600 square miles, or 1,024,000 acres, of which 341,333 acres are cultivated; an equal number is capable of cultivation, and the remaining 341,333 are covered with jungle and hills. The following is the estimated distribution of the cultivated area :—

Rice or paddy	146,334 acres.
Janirah and bajra	88,333 „
Pulses	17,666 „
Vegetables	1,000 „

Fruit	2,000	acres.
Other crops, indigo, &c.	86,000	„

There is but little rice which answers to the *aus* of Bengal. The *aman*, or winter rice, is the universal crop.

The produce of one *bigha*, paying Rs. 1-8 rent, is five maunds of paddy, the value of which is Rs. 5; that of land paying Rs. 3, is 9 maunds, the value of which would be Rs. 9. No second crops are obtained from such land, with the exception of wheat and *khesari*, and in this District only in very rare cases. A fair produce from the former would be 1½ maunds, and from the latter 2 maunds; the value of which would be Rs. 1-8 and Rs. 2 respectively.

AGRICULTURAL POPULATION.—The Assistant Commissioner has not furnished me with any information on this subject, neither does the Census Report of 1872 detail the population according to Occupation separately, for each of the sub-districts of the Santál Parganás. I therefore take the agricultural and labouring population from the Census Report for the entire District of the Santál Parganás.

The total "Agricultural and Pastoral Castes" of the District of the Santál Parganás, as ascertained by the Census of 1872 (pp. cxxvii., cxxviii.), amounts to 118,515, including males, females, and children, and exclusive of Musalmáns, aborigines, or semi-aborigines, wholly or partly living by agriculture. But by analysing the details of population arranged according to Occupation (pp. clxix., clxx.), I find that the total male adults of class iv., *i.e.*, persons engaged in agriculture or with animals, is 205,977. Allowing two other persons as an average of females and children connected with each male adult, the total population living by agriculture or by tending animals amounts to 617,931. Deducting 1004 male adults for the "excepted classes," explained at a foregoing page, *i.e.*, persons possessing estates or otherwise well off, a balance remains of 204,973 males, or allowing two persons to each male adult, a total population of 614,919 souls living by actual husbandry or employed in connection with animals, or tenure-holders belonging to classes who are often people in a small way. This may be taken as the *gross* agricultural population. The total number of male adult "cultivators" as returned by the Census is 201,456, or taking the average of two males to each male adult for women and children, a *net* cultivating population of 604,368.

The male adults employed in cultivation form about one-third of the total males of the District; and the total number of males, females, and children living by cultivation (as obtained by allowing two other persons to each male adult) amounts to 604,368, or about one-half of the total population of the District (1,259,287).

LABOURING POPULATION.—The Census Report in its Statement of Castes and Nationalities returns the labouring classes, below the rank of artisans, of the Santál Parganás District, as follow. Some of the figures have been corrected from the subsequent District Census Statements compiled by Mr C. F. Magrath.

The discrepancy between the results obtained from the Caste and Occupation Statements probably arises from the fact that a large proportion of the aboriginal or semi-aboriginal tribes (who are here entered as labourers) are in reality cultivators. But they form the lowest class of husbandmen, and on the approach of famine abandon their fields to seek hired labour, and are thus thrown on the labouring population.

1. Aborigines	557,277
2. Semi-Hinduised aborigines	224,312
3. Personal servant castes	48,182
4. Weaver castes	9,987
5. Labouring castes	6,927
6. Boating and fishing castes	9,664
7. Beggar and vagabond castes	701
8. Unclassified, Vaishnavs, &c.	9,668
Total ...	866,718

Turning to the Statement of Occupations (pp. clxv.-clxxix.), I find the following numbers under their respective classes. I only take those who may fairly be considered in the rank of labouring men:—

		MALE ADULTS.
Class I. (*Government employ*)	Píyádás	23
Class II. (*Professionals*)	Musicians	753
Class III. *Service.*	Personal servants ...	4,724
	Sweepers	112
	Water-carriers ...	31
	Unspecified ...	7,610

Class	Occupation		Number
Class V. *Conveyance of goods.*	Cartmen ...	...	674
	Bullock-drivers	...	89
	Palki-bearers	...	438
	Boatmen ...	...	1,221
Class VI. *Poorer craftsmen.*	Lime-burners	...	14
	Basket-makers	...	466
	Cotton-spinners	...	2,680
	Cotton-carders	...	120
Class VII. *Miscellaneous.*	Beggars ...	...	1,360
	Labourers ...	...	49,354
	Unemployed	...	50,369
	Total	...	120,038

The total population of the Santál Parganás is 1,259,287. Taken by castes, therefore, there are 866,844 persons belonging to the labouring classes, or two-thirds of the total population. According to occupation, there are 120,038 male adults, or allowing two other persons to each, 360,114 males, females, and children, being more than three-tenths of the total population.

The foregoing calculations yield the following net results :—

1. Total population	1,259,287
2. Agriculturists according to caste statement (Hindus)	118,515
3. Agriculturists according to occupation (all)	614,919
4. Labouring population according to caste statement (Hindus, aborigines, &c.)	866,718
5. Labouring population according to occupation (all)	360,114
6. Total agriculturists and labourers according to caste statement (Hindus, aborigines, &c.)	985,233
7. Total agriculturists and labourers according to occupation (all)	975,033

N.B.—It must be remembered that the totals of agricultural and labouring population according to occupation are obtained by multiplying the *male adults* by 3.

KUCH BEHAR DIVISION.

JALPAIGURI DISTRICT.

The famine of 1866 hardly affected Jalpáigurí District. A considerable quantity of grain, however, was exported to other Districts, which raised the price of rice to about double its ordinary rates. In 1870 the ordinary prices of rice food grains were returned to me by the Dy. Commissioner at Re. 1 to Rs. 1-8 a maund for common rice in ordinary use, and common paddy from 8 to 12 annas a maund.

Famine Warnings. — The Dy. Commissioner reports that prices may be considered to have reached famine rates when rice sells at 8 to 10 seers for the rupee, or from Rs. 4 to Rs. 5 a maund, and is of opinion that relief operations would then become necessary. Jalpáigurí District mainly depends for its food supply on *aman* or cold-weather harvest. If a total loss of the *aus* or autumn rice harvest took place, it would not be very much felt; but in the event of a total destruction of the *aman* crop, the loss could not be compensated for by the *aus* harvest, and the Collector reports that he would apprehend a famine. The people in the Western Dwárs portion of the District find abundance of common vegetables and wild fruits in the jungles which they cook as food, and also numerous varieties of berries which they eat, and in the event of a famine they would be much better off than the people in the regularly-settled parts where the land is more cultivated.

Means of Transit.—There are several fair roads and numerous navigable rivers and streams in the District, which are reported to afford sufficient facilities for importation, as to prevent the danger of any particular part of the District being isolated in the event of a famine. The Deputy Commissioner stated that famine in Jalpáigurí is not at all likely to occur. Being bounded on the north throughout its entire length by the lofty Bhutan range, he thought it very improbable that either the local rainfall, or the supply of water brought down by the rivers and streams, would be affected by even the severest drought which might occur in other Districts.

Out-turn of Crops. — The Deputy Commissioner has not given me any statistics of the area under cultivation, but thinks that fully three-fourths of the total area of the District are cultivated, and that three-fourths of the remaining one-fourth are capable of being brought under tillage. He roughly estimated in 1870 the proportion of land under rice to be 10-16ths of the total cultivated area, and that under other food grains at 1-16th of the total cultivated area; the remaining 5-16ths being under oil seeds, cotton, jute, and tobacco, or occupied as homestead sites or garden-land. A fair average yield from a *bigha* of *aus* rice-land was returned by the Deputy Commissioner at from 8 to 10 maunds of paddy, worth, according to quality of the grain and to the time of the year, from Rs. 4-8 to Rs. 9. A fair out-turn from land growing *aman* or winter rice would be from 10 to 12 maunds of paddy, worth from 12 annas to Rs. 1-4 a maund, the average value of the produce being about Rs. 11 a *bigha*.

Agricultural Population.—The Deputy Commissioner was unable to give any statistics as to the proportion of agriculturists to the labouring population of Jalpáigurí. He stated, however, in his report, that of the indigenous population of the District, he believes that 49 out of every 50 persons were either entirely or partially dependent on agriculture for their livelihood.

The Census Report of 1872 (p. cxviii.) returns the total "Agricultural and Pastoral Castes" (Hindus) of the Jalpáigurí District at 153,353 males, females, and children; inclusive of the semi-Hinduised aboriginals, who in this part of the country are chiefly cultivators, but exclusive of Musalmáns and aborigines partly living by agriculture. Analysing the details of population arranged according to occupation (pp. cxlv., cxlvi.), I find that the total male adults of class iv., *i.e.*, persons engaged in agriculture or with animals, is 82,535. Allowing two other individuals as an average for females and children connected with each male adult, the total population living by agriculture or by tending animals amounts to 247,605. Deducting 295 male adults for the "excepted classes" explained at a previous page (*i.e.*, persons possessing estate or otherwise well off), a balance remains of 82,240 males under class iv.; or allowing two other persons to each male adult, a total population of 246,720 living by actual husbandry or employed in connection with animals, or tenure-holders belonging to the classes who are generally people in a small way. This may be taken as the *gross* agricultural population. The total number of male adult "cultivators" as returned by the Census is 82,128, or allowing an average of two persons to each male adult as family and children, a total net "cultivating" population of 246,384.

The male adults employed in cultivation form about half of the total males in the District; and the total number of males, females, and children living by cultivation (as obtained by allowing two other individuals to each male adult) amounts to 246,384 (exclusive of the Dwárs, for which the Census does not furnish these details), or about three-fifths of the total population of the District (418,665).

The Census Report in its Statement of Castes and Nationalities (pp. cxli.–cxlvii.) returns the labouring classes, below the rank of artisans, of the Jalpáigurí District, thus:—

1. Aboriginal tribes	553
2. Personal servant castes	4,373
3. Weaver castes	5,685
4. Labouring castes	306
5. Boating and fishing castes	1,656
6. Musicians and vagabond castes	280
7. Unclassified, Vaishnavs, &c.	4,876
Total ...	17,729

Turning to the Statement of Occupations (p. cxli.–clvii.), I find the following numbers under the five classes. I only take those who may be fairly considered in the rank of labouring men, and exclusive of the Dwárs:—

		MALE ADULTS.
Class II. (*Professionals*)	Musicians	903
Class III. *Service.*	Personal servants ...	1,163
	Sweepers	72
	Water-carriers	29
	Unspecified	1,972
Class V. *Conveyance of goods.*	Cartmen	66
	Bullock-drivers	7
	Palki-bearers	317
	Boatmen	194

Class	Occupation	Number
Class VI. *Poorer craftsmen.*	Basket-makers	8
	Weavers in cotton ...	1,283
	Shoe-makers	26
Class VII. *Miscellaneous.*	Beggars	1,241
	Labourers	942
	Unemployed	295
	Total ...	11,218

The total population of the District is 418,665. Taken by castes, therefore, there are 17,729 persons belonging to labouring classes, or about one twenty-fourth part of the total population. According to occupation, there are 11,218 male adults who may fairly be considered in the rank of labouring men, or 33,654 males, females, and children, comprising about one-thirteenth part of the total population. The discrepancy between the results obtained from the Caste and Occupation Statements probably arises from the fact that a portion of the semi-aboriginal castes (who are here as a tribe chiefly cultivators, and are entered as such) employ themselves as hired labourers.

The foregoing calculations give the following net results. The details are exclusive of the Dwárs:—

1. Total population	418,665
2. Hindu agriculturists according to caste statement	153,353
3. Total agriculturists according to occupation statement	246,720
4. Labourers (Hindus), aborigines, &c., according to caste	17,729
5. Total labourers according to occupation ...	33,654
6. Total of agriculturists and labourers (Hindus), aborigines, &c.	177,082
7. Total of agriculturists and labourers (all) according to occupation	280,374

N.B.—It must be remembered that the total of agriculturists and labourers, according to occupation, is obtained by multiplying the number of male adults by three. The figures have been corrected from the subsequent District Census Statements. Nos. 2 to 7 are exclusive of the Dwárs, for which no details exist.

GOALPARA DISTRICT.

FAMINES.—The Dy. Commissioner, in his report dated January 1871, stated that, in the strict sense of the word, there was no famine in Goálpárá District in 1866, and accordingly has not furnished a return of food prices for that year. The ordinary rates in 1871 were returned as follow:—Best quality rice and paddy, Rs. 5 and Rs. 2-4 a maund; common rice and paddy, Rs. 1-8 and 12 annas a maund respectively. High prices prevailed during 1866, but they were mainly caused by the demand in other Districts.

FAMINE WARNINGS.—The Dy. Commissioner thinks prices should be considered to have reached the famine rate when coarse rice sells as high as Rs. 7-8 a maund, or 5⅓ seers for the rupee, and that relief operations on the part of Government would then become necessary. The cheapest sort of rice selling at Rs. 5 a maund, or 8 seers per rupee, with the produce of the total *aus* and *aman* crops at less than 5-8ths of an average harvest, would be a warning of approaching famine. Goálpárá District chiefly depends upon the *aman* crop, but a considerable amount of *aus* is also grown, and the Collector reported to me that the total failure of either one of these crops could not be compensated by a good out-turn from the other.

MEANS OF TRANSIT.—The Brahmaputra affords the principal means of communication, but there are other rivers also navigable by steamers and large boats. The Dy. Commissioner thinks that in case of famine the rivers would afford sufficient means for importation, although roads or a railway are also needed. The only suggestion made by the Dy. Commissioner as to remedial or mitigating measures during famine, is the importation of grain from other Districts, and the establishment of relief depots at Dhubrí, Mániker-char, Lakshmípur, and Goálpárá.

AREA UNDER CULTIVATION; OUT-TURN OF CROPS.—The area of the District was returned by the Dy. Commissioner in 1871 at 1,832,320 acres, of which a little under one-third, or 588,768 acres, were said to be cultivated; 265,600 acres uncultivated, but capable of being brought under tillage; and the remaining 977,952 acres jungle and waste. The comparative acreage under the principal crops was thus returned in 1871:—Rice, 404,778 acres; wheat, 300 acres; mustard seed, 73,696 acres; jute, not known; other crops, 115,994 acres.

Out-turn of Crops.—A fair yield from *aus* land is said to be 7 maunds of paddy per *bigha*, worth about Re. 1 per maund; and from *aman* land about 8½ maunds of paddy, of an average value of Rs. 1-4 a maund. In *aus* lands, a second crop of mustard is sown after the autumn harvest, the average out-turn being 3 maunds a *bigha*, worth about Rs. 1-12 a maund. The total value of the produce of a *bigha* of *aus* land growing two crops (the early rice and the mustard) is returned at Rs. 12-4, and that of a *bigha* of *aman* land growing both the early and winter rice crops is returned at Rs. 8-6.

Agriculturists.—The Dy. Commissioner gives no statistics regarding the proportion of the agricultural and labouring population. But the Census Report of 1872 (p. cxxxix.) gives the total "Agricultural, Pastoral, and Semi-aboriginal Castes" of the Goálpárá District at 149,143, including males, females, and children; but exclusive of the Musalmáns and aboriginal castes partly or wholly living by agriculture. I have taken the semi-Hinduised aboriginal tribes among the agriculturists, as in this part of the country they chiefly live by cultivation. The figures taken from the Census Report have been corrected from the District Census Statement subsequently drawn up. By analysing the details of population at pp. clxix., clxx., I find that the total male adults of class iv., *i.e.*, persons engaged in agriculture or with animals, is 102,838. Allowing two other persons as an average for females and children connected with each male adult, the total population living by agriculture or by tending animals amounts to 308,514. Deducting 185 male adults for the "excepted classes" explained at a foregoing page (*i.e.*, persons possessing estates or otherwise well off), a balance remains of 102,653 males under class iv.; or allowing two other persons to each male adult, a total population of 307,959 living by actual husbandry or employed in connection with animals, or tenure-holders belonging to the classes who are generally people in a small way. This may be taken as the *gross* agricultural population, but does not include the aboriginal tribes, a large proportion of whom live by husbandry, but who are included in the labouring castes for reasons stated below. The total number of male adult "cultivators" as returned by the Census is 102,080, or allowing an average of two souls to each male adult as family and children, a total *net* cultivating population of 306,240.

The male adults employed in cultivation form about one-half of the total males in the District; and the total number of males, females, and children living by cultivation (as obtained by allowing two other persons to each male adult) amounts to 306,240, or about three-fourths of the total population of the District (407,714, according to the District Statements).

LABOURING POPULATION.—The Census Report in its Statement of Castes and Nationalities (pp. cxxxviii.-cxl.) returns the labouring classes, below the rank of artisans, thus.

I have included the aborigines under the labouring castes, although a very large proportion of them live by agriculture. But they are the poorest and most improvident class of cultivators, the class whose husbandry first breaks down under a famine, and who are forced to seek a subsistence by labour, and are thus thrown upon the labouring population.

1. Aboriginal tribes	97,732
2. Personal servant castes	2,798
3. Weaver castes	15,119
4. Labouring castes	9,472
5. Boating and fishing castes	24,653
6. Musician and vagabond castes	275
7. Unspecified, Vaishnavs, &c.	4053
Total ...	154,102

Turning to the Statement of Occupations (pp. clxv.-clxxix.), I find the following numbers under their respective classes. I only take those who may fairly be considered in the rank of labouring men:—

		MALE ADULTS.
Class I. (*Govt. employ*)	Píyádás	5
Class II. (*Professionals*)	Musicians	237
Class III. *Service.*	Personal servants ...	8,701
	Sweepers	149
	Water-carriers ...	16
	Unspecified ...	2,139
Class V. *Conveyance of goods.*	Boatmen	632

Class VI. *Poorer sorts of craftsmen.*	Cotton-spinners	...	230
Class VII.	Beggars ...	...	1,897
	Labourers ...	...	3,722
	Unemployed	...	1,067
	Total	...	18,795

Total population, according to the District Statements, 407,714. Taken by castes, therefore, there are 154,102 persons belonging to labouring classes, or above one-third of the total population. According to occupation, there are 18,795 male adults who may fairly be considered the rank of labouring men, or 56,385 males, females, and children, comprising about one-seventh of the total population. The discrepancy between the result obtained from the Caste and Occupation Statements probably arises from the fact that a large proportion of the aboriginal tribes, weaver and fishing castes (who are here entered as belonging to the rank of labourers), are in reality either cultivators or fishermen. But they are generally poor people, and on the approach of a famine migrate or abandon their profession to seek hired labour, and would thus be thrown on the labouring population.

The foregoing calculations give, therefore, the following net results. I take the figures from the subsequent District Compilation. It does not exactly appear whether the Eastern Dwárs are included. The original Census Report gave a total population of 444,761 :—

1. Total population	407,714
2. Agriculturists (Hindus) and semi-aboriginals according to caste statement ...	149,143
3. Agriculturists (total) according to occupation statement	307,959
4. Labouring (Hindus and aborigines) according to caste	154,102
5. Labourers (total) according to occupation	56,385
6. Total of agriculturists and labourers according to caste statement	303,245
7. Total of agriculturists and labourers according to occupation statement	364,344

N.B.—It should always be remembered that the occupation totals are obtained by multiplying the male adults by three, and that this proportion is perhaps a little too high.

DARJILING DISTRICT.

FAMINE PRICES.—The maximum price of rice throughout the Dárjiling District during the Bengal famine of 1866, as returned by the Deputy Commissioner in a report dated April 1871, was 5 seers for the rupee, or Rs. 8 per maund for the dearest sort, and 8 seers for the rupee, or Rs. 5 a maund for the cheapest sort. At the time of the Deputy Commissioner's report, April 1871, prices were said to have reverted to their ordinary rates.

FAMINE WARNINGS.—Dárjiling District consists of two distinct tracts having very different physical features, a hilly portion known as the *morang*, and a *tarai* of undulating plains at the foot of the hills. The hill division is very scantily populated, and the Deputy Commissioner in 1871 reported that the means of earning a livelihood were so easy that it was difficult to conceive the possibility of famine in this tract. There would be no danger so long as there was no famine in the *tarai* or Districts to the south, but if prices rose steadily so as to reach 8 seers of Indian corn or rice for the rupee, or Rs. 5 a maund, the Deputy Commissioner reported that he would send notice of the rise in prices to Sikim, Nepál, and to the Districts on the plains, and also make inquiries regarding edible jungle vegetable and fruits. In reply to the Deputy Commissioner's inquiries, several intelligent hill-men asserted that rice or Indian corn selling at 5 seers for the rupee, or Rs. 8 a maund, would be considered a famine price; but the Deputy Commissioner was of opinion that the hill population would have migrated to other localities long before prices reached this rate. One warning of famine in the hills would be the failure of the *bara* or winter rice crop, upon which, together with Indian corn and imported rice, the people chiefly depend.

In the *tarai* or lowland division of the District, the Deputy Commissioner reported that if paddy were selling at Rs. 3-5 a maund, famine rates would be reached. These prices would indicate a general failure of the crop throughout the *tarai* and in the neighbouring Districts. The Deputy Commissioner reported that Government would then have to step in by importing rice, and employing the people on local relief works, such as roads, to enable them to purchase grain. A failure of the lowland rice would be an indication of approaching famine. If the price of paddy ranged high in December or January soon after the harvest, and showed signs of rapidly rising above Rs. 1-5 a maund, the Deputy Commissioner reported that he would anticipate a famine later in the year. The Dárjiling *tarai* depends chiefly upon the lowland rice crop, and so long as that is good or even yields an average crop there is no fear of famine.

The Means of Transit at the disposal of the District are not sufficient, in the opinion of the Deputy Commissioner, to avert famine by importations, and in the event of a general famine throughout Bengal, Dárjiling would suffer severely. The principal road is that from Caragola, but in 1871 it was reported as in an indifferent state, with many important bridges on it giving way every year in the rains. This road would not suffice for rapid importations. The hill people would not be likely to suffer very much, as they would migrate to where they could obtain yams or other edible roots, if they could not get better food. But to save the *tarai* from danger of famine, the Deputy Commissioner reported that it must first be connected with the seaboard by means of a railway. This work has now been sanctioned by the Viceroy, and orders have been issued for the vigorous prosecution of the undertaking (1873).

Cultivated Area; Out-turn of Crops.—The total area of the hill division of the District was returned by the Deputy Commissioner in 1871 at 615,321 acres, of which only 22,453 acres were cultivated; 456,945 acres were returned as cultivable, but not under tillage; while the remaining 135,923 acres were uncultivable and waste. The estimated acreage under the different crops was reported by the Deputy Commissioner to be as follows:—Rice, 6147 acres; *mahua*, 4083 acres; Indian corn, 2233 acres; oil seeds, 40 acres; potatoes, 174 acres; tea, 9000 acres; cinchona, 300 acres; vegetables, 11 acres; fruit trees, 3 acres; cotton, 58 acres; other crops, 404 acres; total, 22,453 acres. The Deputy Commissioner stated in his report that, in his opinion, a *bigha* of land in the Dárjiling hills, favourably situated and cultivated by a Nepalese husbandman, would yield as much paddy as a *bigha* of the best land in the other hills, namely, from five to six maunds a *bigha*. In good years after harvest-time, paddy in the hills can be obtained at the rate of one and a half maunds per rupee, and if payment is made in advance, at even two maunds per rupee. It is not usual to grow a second crop, but occasionally wheat is grown after the rice harvest has been gathered in, on the same land. A fair average value of the produce of a *bigha* in the hills is returned by the Deputy Commissioner at from Rs. 5 to Rs. 6.

The total area of the *tarai* or lowland division of the District is returned at 173,856 acres, of which 62,115 acres were returned by the Deputy Commissioner in 1871 as under cultivation; 100,875 acres as cultivable, but not under tillage; and the remaining 10,866 acres as uncultivable and waste. The estimated acreage under the different crops was returned by the Deputy Commissioner as follows:—Rice, 47,737 acres; cotton, 3818 acres; pulses, 1909 acres; jute, 3818 acres; oil seeds, 1324 acres; sugar cane, 1409 acres; tea, 1900 acres; vegetables, 50 acres; fruit trees, 50 acres; other crops, 100 acres; total, 62,115 acres. The Deputy Commissioner reported to me that a good average crop is about six maunds of paddy per *bigha*. The paddy, if sold at the time of harvesting, will fetch only at the rate of one and a half maunds per rupee, but if kept back for some time it is worth at least Re. 1 per maund. No second crops are grown on rice-lands in the *tarai*.

AGRICULTURAL POPULATION.—The Collector has furnished me with no particulars regarding the proportion of agriculturists to labourers. But the Census Report of 1872 (pp. cxvii., cxviii.) gives the total "Agricultural, Pastoral, and semi-Hinduised Aboriginal Castes" of the Dárjiling District at 26,593, including males, females, and children, but exclusive of Musalmáns and aborigines living by agriculture. Adding to this the 25,781 Nepalese who chiefly live by cultivation, the total of cultivating population according to Caste Statement amounts to 52,374 males, females, and children. The figures have been corrected from the subsequent District Census Statements, compiled by Mr C. F. Magrath. By analysing the details of population arranged according to occupation (pp. cxlv., cxlvi.), I find that the total male adults of class iv., *i.e.*, persons engaged in agriculture or with animals, amounts to 20,134. Allowing two other individuals as an average of females and children connected with each male adult, the total population living by agriculture or by tending animals amounts to 60,402. Deducting 847 male adults for the "excepted classes" explained at foregoing page, *i.e.*, persons possessing estates or otherwise well off, a balance remains of 19,287 males under class iv., or allowing two other persons to each male adult, a total population of 57,861 souls living by husbandry or employed in connection with animals, or tenure-holders belonging to classes who are often people in a small way. This may be taken as the *gross* agricultural population. The total number of male adult "cultivators" as returned by the Census is 18,936, or taking the average of two persons to each male adult as women and children, a *net* cultivating population of 56,808.

The male adults employed in agriculture form above one-third of the total males in the District, and the total number of males, females, and children living by cultivation (as obtained by allowing two other persons to each male adult) amounts to 56,808, or about three-fifths of the total population (94,712.)

Labouring Population.—The Census Report in its Statement of Castes and Nationalities (pp. cxii.–cxxv.) returns the labouring classes, below the rank of artisans, of the Dárjiling District as follows. The figures have been corrected from the subsequent District Census Statements:—

1. Aboriginal tribes	14,088
2. Personal servant castes	614
3. Weaver castes	1,701
4. Labouring castes	86
5. Boating and fishing castes	81
6. Beggar and vagabond castes	14
7. Unspecified, Vaishnavs, &c.	5,119
Total ...	21,703

Turning to the Statement of Occupations (pp. cxli.–clvii.), I find the following numbers under their respective classes. I only take those who may fairly be considered in the rank of labouring men:—

		MALE ADULTS.
Class I. (*Government employ*)	Píyádás ...	109
Class II. (*Professionals*)	Musicians ...	9

Class III. *Service.*	Personal servants ...	702
	Sweepers	88
	Water-carriers	22
	Unspecified	42
Class V. *Conveyance of goods.*	Palki-bearers	61
	Boatmen	8
Class VI. *Poorer craftsmen.*	Basket-makers	33
	Weavers	303
	Shoe-makers	40
Class VII. *Miscellaneous.*	Beggars	168
	Labourers	10,131
	Unemployed	306
	Total ...	12,022

The total population of the District is 94,712. Taken by castes, therefore, there are 21,703 persons belonging to labouring classes, or about two-ninths of the total population. According to occupation, there are 12,022 male adults, or 36,066 males, females, and children, or about two-fifths of the total population. The difference between the number of labourers as taken according to Caste, and that taken according to Occupation Statement, is owing, perhaps, to the large number of coolies employed in the tea-gardens being returned under their castes, which do not always belong to the rank of labouring classes, and hence are not included in my statement of labourers according to caste.

The foregoing calculations give, therefore, the following net results :—

1.	Total population	94,712
2.	Agriculturists (Hindus, &c.) according to caste statement	52,374
3.	Agriculturists (total) according to occupation	57,861
4.	Labourers (Hindus and aborigines) according to caste	21,703
5.	Labourers (total) according to occupation ...	36,066
6.	Total of (Hindu, &c.) agriculturists and labourers according to caste statement ...	74,077
7.	Total of (all) agriculturists and labourers according to occupation	93,927

N.B.—It must be remembered that the total of agriculturists and labourers according to occupation is obtained by multiplying the *male adults* by three.

GARO HILLS DISTRICT.

THE Gáro Hills District was not affected by the famine of 1866.

FAMINE WARNINGS.—The Deputy Commissioner, in his report to me, dated March 1871, stated that the staple product of the Gáro Hills is rice, of which only one crop is grown in the year. Rice is not grown as an article of trade, but merely for local consumption, and large stocks of grain are never kept in hand. Consequently the only warning of famine in the Gáro Hills, would be the advent of the calamity itself. The price of grain would be no guide, as rice is not commonly bought or sold. The Deputy Commissioner states that he would consider anything likely to cause the failure of the current year's crop to be a warning of scarcity, as the people of the Gáro Hills do not generally keep sufficient stores to enable them to tide over the total loss of one season's crops. Unless famine were also general in the surrounding Districts of the plains, however, the Deputy Commissioner would not apprehend any serious distress. As a rule, the Gáros have some money, and are close to the plains, where, even if moneyless, they can easily earn a livelihood. Want of rain throughout March, April, and May would mean an almost total loss of the crops, and if prolonged a little later in the season, the failure of the crops would be complete. In the event of a local famine, and if supplies could not be obtained from the neighbouring Districts, the Deputy Commissioner is of opinion that it would be necessary to provide large relief centres at the hill passes, as the distress would then be universal. Strong guards would also be required at the passes for the protection of the people of the plains from raids by the hill-men. The Deputy Commissioner does not think that any other measures could be taken.

OUT-TURN OF CROPS.—An average out-turn from a *bigha* of rice-land is roughly estimated at two maunds, valued at about Rs. 2-8. It must, however, be borne in mind that the Gáros cultivate only for their own consumption. The value given here is, therefore, calculated according to the probable cost of buying paddy at the nearest markets, whence in a case of a bad harvest it would be necessary to procure supplies, than on any actual local rates.

The Deputy Commissioner of the District has not furnished me with any particulars regarding the proportion of agriculturists to labourers, nor does the Census Report of 1872 detail the population according to caste, nationality, or occupation.

KUCH BEHAR STATE.

FAMINE PRICES.—The Deputy Commissioner, in his report of April 1871, states that the maximum price of paddy and rice during the famine of 1866 was Rs. 4-12 and Rs. 6 a maund respectively. Local prices had in 1871 returned to what was formerly considered ordinary rates. In 1866 the scarcity did not amount to a famine, as it was not necessary for the State to afford relief. The scarcity of 1854 really amounted to famine, although the prices which prevailed that year were less than those which were current in 1866. In the latter year, however, the people were in a much more prosperous condition, and consequently felt the scarcity less keenly.

FAMINE WARNINGS.—The Deputy Commissioner reported in 1871, that when ordinary rice rises from Rs. 5 to Rs. 6 a maund it may be considered a famine rate. If in January and February the price of rice reaches Rs. 3 a maund, the Deputy Commissioner would consider it a warning of famine later in the year. If a total loss of the *aus* crop took place it would not be much felt, but if the *aman* entirely failed, the Deputy Commissioner reported that there would be danger of a famine.

COMMUNICATIONS. — The roads and numerous rivers afford, in the Deputy Commissioner's opinion, sufficient facilities for importation, as to prevent danger of isolation of any particular part of the State in time of famine. Carts and pack-bullocks can travel all over the State in the cold weather, in places even where there are no roads.

AREA OF CULTIVATION; OUT-TURN OF CROPS.—The total area

of the State was returned in 1871 at 832,129 acres, of which there are under cultivation about 645,951 acres. Jhils, tanks, creeks, and rivers take up about 61,071 acres more; the remainder is covered with jungle, about 3-4ths of which are considered capable of being cultivated. The area under rice in 1871 was estimated at 3-4ths of the total cultivated area of the State.

From 8 to 10 maunds per *bigha* are considered a fair yield for first-class rice-lands, and from 4 to 6 maunds for the worst clays, the paddy being worth from 12 annas to Re. 1 a maund, besides the straw, which will fetch from about 12 annas to Re. 1 per *bigha*, or a sum of Rs. 8-12 and 5-4 respectively, for the total out-turn. Sometimes two crops of rice, one of *aus* and one of *aman*, are obtained from the same land during the year, and occasionally pulses are also sown on the *aman* land. The value of the second crops varies from Rs. 2 to 5 a *bigha*, which raises the mean value of the two different sorts of lands to Rs. 12-4 and Rs. 8-12 per standard *bigha*.

The Deputy Commissioner of Kuch Behar has not furnished me with any information regarding the proportion of agriculturists to labourers, and the Census having been taken at the time of last Settlement, no details of population as to caste, nationality, or occupation are given in the Census Report of 1872.

RAJSHAHI DIVISION.

RAJSHAHI DISTRICT.

Famine Prices.—The Collector of Rájsháhí states that famine prices in 1866-67 were 8 seers of rice and 12 seers of paddy for the rupee. Government relief operations, however, were not needed; local prices at date of the Collector's report (April 1871) had returned to their ordinary rates before the famine.

Famine Warnings.—The Collector is of opinion that preparations for relief operations are necessary when the prices of food, having reached those of 1866-67, show the slightest tendency to rise. If rice should sell at 16 seers a rupee in January or February after the winter harvest, the Collector considers it ought to be taken as a warning of famine later in the year. The District depends chiefly on *aman* and *ropa* rice, which are both winter crops. The *aus* or autumn crop could not make up for an almost total loss of the *aman* harvest, nor could the autumn crop alone, even if a plentiful one, enable the people to live through the year without actual famine.

Means of Transit.—The Collector in his report to me states that if exportation from the District ceased in seasons of scarcity, the people might escape famine without importation from other Districts; but a cessation of exports is not to be expected; and should the District be brought to depend entirely on imported grain, the Collector expressed his doubts as to whether sufficient facilities for importation were at his disposal, especially between the months of April and July, as there are no railways in the District, very few roads suitable for traffic, and the rivers and canals dry up in the summer when the scarcity of food is most to be apprehended.

Cultivated Area; Out-turn of Crops.—The area of the

District was returned by the Collector in 1871 at 3002 square miles, of which 1523 were under cultivation; the remaining 1479 square miles being uncultivated, partly cultivable and partly uncultivable. The following is an estimate of the comparative acreage devoted to principal crops:—Rice, 97,452 acres; peas, *khesari*, and oil seeds, 20,000 acres; indigo, 10,000 acres; mulberry, 8981 acres; *ganja*, 5500 acres. Nine maunds of paddy are considered a fair yield per *bigha*, the value of which is estimated at Rs. 5 to Rs. 6. In the Nator portion of the District, the rice-lands produce second crops in abundance, such as *khesari*, peas, oil seeds, &c., the yield of which is from 2 to 3 maunds per *bigha*, valued at Rs. 3 to Rs. 4.

AGRICULTURAL POPULATION. — The Collector has furnished me with no particulars regarding the proportion of agriculturists to labourers. But the Census Report of 1872 (pp. cxviii., cxix.) gives the total "Agricultural and Pastoral Castes" (Hindus) of the Rájsháhí District at 75,331, including males, females, and children; and exclusive of Musalmáns who live by agriculture, and of the aboriginal and semi-aboriginal castes partly living by cultivation. But by analysing the details of population arranged according to occupation at pp. cxli.–clvii., I find that the total male adults of class iv., *i.e.*, persons engaged in tillage or with animals, number 241,784. Allowing two other persons as an average for females and children connected with each male adult, the total population living by agriculture or by tending animals amounts to 725,352. Deducting 3201 male adults for the "excepted classes," as explained at a previous page, *i.e.*, persons possessing estates or otherwise well off, a balance remains of 238,583 males under class iv.; or allowing two other persons to each male adult, a total population of 715,749 souls living by husbandry or employed in connection with animals, or tenure-holders belonging to classes who are often people in a small way. The total number of male adult "cultivators" as returned by the Census is 234,030; or taking the average of two souls to each male adult for women and children, a *net* cultivating population of 702,090.

The male adults directly employed in cultivation form about three-eighths of the total males in the District, and the total number of males, females, and children living by cultivation (as estimated by allowing two other persons to each male adult) amounts to 702,090, or about four-sevenths of the total population of the District (1,310,729).

LABOURING POPULATION.—The Census Report in its Statement of Castes and Nationalities (pp. cxiv.–cxxiii.) returns the labouring classes, below the rank of artisans, of the Rájsháhí District, as follow. Some of the figures have been corrected from the District Census Statements, as subsequently compiled by Mr C. F. Magrath:—

1. Aboriginal tribes	7,076
2. Semi-Hinduised aborigines	67,504
3. Personal servant castes	12,192
4. Weaver castes	4,255
5. Labouring castes	4,900
6. Boating and fishing castes	24,016
7. Musicians and vagabond castes	544
8. Unspecified, Vaishnavs, &c.	23,407
Total ...	143,894

Turning to the Statement of Occupations (pp. cxli.–clvii.), I find the following numbers under their respective classes. I only take those who may fairly be considered in the rank of labouring men:—

		MALE ADULTS.
Class I. (*Government employ*)	Píyádás	195
Class II. (*Professionals*)	Musicians	1,956
Class III. *Service.*	Personal servants ...	6,502
	Sweepers	77
	Water-carriers	3
	Unspecified	6,756
Class V. *Conveyance of goods.*	Cartmen	1,466
	Bullock-drivers ...	10
	Palki-bearers	1,508
	Boatmen	7,432
Class VI. *Poorer sorts of craftsmen.*	Brick-makers	17
	Well-diggers	2
	Basket-makers	479
	Cotton-spinners ...	75
	Cotton-carders	6
	Cotton-weavers ...	6,551
	Shoe-makers	416
	Bird-catchers	3

Class VII. *Miscellaneous.*	Beggars	6,825
	Labourers	48,843
	Unemployed	3,033
	Total ...	92,155

The total population of the District is 1,310,729. Taken by castes, therefore, there are 143,894 persons belonging to labouring classes, or more than a ninth of the total population. According to occupation, there are 92,155 male adults who may fairly be considered in the rank of labouring men, or 276,465 males, females, and children, comprising over one-fifth of the total population.

The foregoing calculations give, therefore, the following results:

1. Total population	1,310,729
2. Agriculturists (Hindus) according to caste statement	75,331
3. Agriculturists (total) according to occupation statement	715,749
4. Labourers (Hindus and aborigines) according to caste	143,894
5. Labourers (total) according to occupation	276,465
6. Total Hindu agriculturists and labourers according to caste statement	219,225
7. Total agriculturists and labourers (all) according to occupation statement ...	992,214

N.B.—It should always be remembered that the occupation totals are obtained by multiplying the *male adults* by three.

RANGPUR DISTRICT.

FAMINE PRICES.—The Collector in his report to me, February 1871, states that this District has had no experience of famine, within the memory of the oldest inhabitant, resulting either from inundation or drought. The complaint of the cultivators has more frequently been the too great abundance of rice, and the consequent difficulty in disposing of it at a remunerative price. In 1787-88, however, a famine occurred which necessitated the purchase of 1330 maunds of rice by Government, at a cost of Rs. 2053. The maximum price of grain in 1866 was as follows:—Best cleaned rice, Rs. 5-11 a maund; common rice, Rs. 4-5 a maund.

FAMINE WARNINGS.—In 1871 prices had returned to the ordinary rates prevailing previous to the famine of 1866; the Collector in his report, states that if anything, they were somewhat cheaper. The unusual prices during 1866 caused considerable inconvenience in the District, but the scarcity never amounted to a famine. At the beginning of November, just before the winter harvest, the price of rice had risen to the maximum; that of an ordinary kind selling at eight seers per rupee, while the very cheapest description was as dear as $9\frac{1}{3}$ seers; these prices, however, lasted but a comparatively short time, in consequence of the gathering in of the new crop.

The Collector is of opinion, from the experience of the year 1866, that if in January or February the price of ordinary rice rose as high as eight seers for the rupee, prospects would have become sufficiently serious to justify the intervention of Government. With such rates prevailing, the winter crops must have been very scanty, and the chances of a spring crop very poor. The Collector states that so long as prices remain as high as Rs. 5 a maund, and unless there was an absolute certainty that importation would take place on private account, it would, in his opinion, be the duty of Government to take measures to provide grain for those who would shortly become dependent on State relief.

The Collector thinks that were Government relief operations confined to buying food in the District, and distributing it among the starving, prices would probably be enhanced still farther. The State purchases might induce neighbouring Districts to pour in supplies, but unless certain knowledge existed regarding such stores, and of their becoming available for the District, the Collector considers it would be the duty of Government to import sufficient food from other Districts, to keep prices at an equilibrium till succour could be obtained from more distant Provinces. Were too much imported, prices would fall, and the confidence of the merchants might be shaken, and private enterprise brought to a stop. Were there no importation at all, the scarcity might turn into famine even for the provident portion of the community, and irretrievable disaster might ensue.

The surest signs of approaching famine in the District would be the high price of grain, taken in conjunction with the events of the season. Crime and mendicancy would become more frequent, and the prices of all articles convertible into food by sale would quickly fall. The wages of labour would at the same time diminish, and the Collector would expect, under the circumstances, to see a very considerable emigration to neighbouring parts, where it is stated that labour is dearer and in much demand. The chief food of the people of this District is rice. The agriculturists who raise *aus* rice retain it mostly for their own consumption. The *aman* crop could certainly, even if only a very moderate one, serve for the subsistence of the people in the event of the total loss of the *aus* crop, provided they had not exported the whole surplus stocks. The value of the *aus* crop, if it were a good one, would probably be sufficient to procure food for the people in the event of the total failure of the *aman* harvest. The crops grown, however, being of a very miscellaneous nature, local produce would have to be exchanged for the cheapest form of food obtainable from other Districts.

MEANS OF TRANSIT.—To avert impending famine, the Collector considers that one of two things must be done, and that quickly. Either the food must be taken to the people, or the people to the food, and that in practice both courses would have to be followed, but neither is practicable unless the communication be improved. In certain parts of the District, nothing but disaster could be anticipated. The navigation of the rivers is dangerous, and except in the case of the Tista, Brahmaputra, and Dharlá, is open only during a very short period of the year. In the case of floods, importation, except with such delay as would render it useless, would be impracticable. Not a single road in the District would be passable, as sufficiently proved by their condition during the rains of even ordinary years. The bridges are generally constructed of timber, and are very frail. In a serious inundation, they would be washed away, and the roads being only slightly embanked, and of a sandy soil, would, in all probability, be scarcely traceable. In such an emergency the existence of a high causeway, amply provided with masonry bridges, would mitigate the sufferings of the people. In cases of excessive drought, better road communication would also be valuable. The Collector states that notwithstanding the large surplus revenue of the District, the sum allowed for Public Works hardly suffices to keep up the roads in their original decayed condition. The great safeguard of this District against famine is, he reports, the climate, which is peculiarly favourable to rice cultivation. Rain considered excessive elsewhere causes no harm in Rangpur, and droughts of long continuance are hardly known.

To prevent famine, the first object to be kept in view is, in the Collector's opinion, the increase of the area from which the food-supply of a District is obtained in ordinary years, and to provide for its rapid extension in cases of emergency by means of improved roads and communications, as already explained. The next object to be kept in view should be to decrease the number of useless mouths, by transporting surplus labour to Districts where it might be remuneratively employed, and to diminish the proportion of those incapacitated from labour by disease, by improving the sanitary condition of the District in ordinary years, before the famine comes. It is also suggested that the indigent should be collected into centres of industry, and that the energies of the cultivators should be directed to the production of the most remunerative crops which the land can produce, and persuaded to retain for their own consumption a larger proportion of their produce; in fact, to raise their standard of living so as to leave a margin for them to fall back upon in times of adversity.

The last suggestion the Collector would offer, although he considers it not by any means the least in importance, is the establishment of "Anna Savings Banks" at every Post-Office throughout the District, and refers to the success of a similar institution in Scotland. The Collector remarks that as the poor carry their money about with them, the temptation to spend it would be greatly diminished were they possessed of the means of safely depositing their surplus earnings. The measures suggested would, however, require to have been years in force previous to any emergency like a scarcity. As the main obstacle to taking proper measures in the case of actually impending famine is the difficulty of attaining correct information in Districts where the cultivators are in communication with the superior landholders only, and Government officials have hardly any opportunities of becoming acquainted with their wants, the Collector suggests that it would be highly desirable to warn all landholders of their duties towards their tenantry, and to impose heavy penalties in cases of death by famine occurring on their lands, unless they could show that there had been no failure on their part to give timely notice of impending want. It must be borne in mind that I merely reproduce the Collector's views without endorsing them. Most of his remedial measures belong to the general improvement of the country in ordinary times, rather than to the direct mitigation of suffering during famine.

OUT-TURN OF CROPS.—The productive qualities of the soil, as regards paddy, vary so much throughout the District, and the rates of rent are so arbitrary and unequal in different *parganas*, that only a very rough calculation can be given of the produce of rice lands. Paddy land rated at Rs. 1-8 a *bigha* is in this District generally known as *ek khanda*, *i.e.*, will produce but one crop in the course of the year. The out-turn would be from 6 to 7 standard maunds per *bigha*, value about Rs. 4. Land rated at Rs. 3 would be of the better sort, producing two crops in the year. These might both be rice, the one the *aus* or autumn crop, and the other the *aman* or winter harvest. In this case the total out-turn in the course of the year would be from 11 to 12 maunds of paddy, worth Rs. 7 or Rs. 7-8. It might, however, be a mixed crop, instead of entirely paddy. On high dry lands, after the removal of a crop of early rice, a fair out-turn of which would be about 4 maunds of paddy, value Rs. 2-8, a second crop can be obtained, consisting of one or other of the following crops:—

Mustard,	2 maunds per *bigha*,	Rs. 3 a md.,	value	Rs.	6	0
Khesari,	3½ „	Rs. 2 4	per maund	... „	7	14
Wheat,	2½ „	„ 3 0	„	... „	7	8
Tobacco,	4½ „	„ 4 8	„	... „	20	4
Musuri,	2½ „	„ 2 8	„	... „	6	4

By a proper selection of soil and care in cultivation, the produce of certain crops, such as sugar-cane, tobacco, jute, and ginger, may be made very remunerative. The Collector estimated that the following out-turn per *bigha* can be obtained under favourable circumstances:—

Unrefined sugar,	9 maunds, value	...	... Rs.	36	0
Refined sugar	3 „	...	... „	60	0
Treacle	4½ „	...	... „	13	8

Tobacco	8 maunds, value	... ... Rs.	36	8
Jute	15 "	... ... "	45	0
Ginger undried	25 "	... ... "	18	0
Ginger (dried)		... ... "	40	0
Turmeric	5½ "	... ... "	22	0
Potatoes	25 "	... ... "	50	0
Betel-nut	13 "	... ... "	39	0
Millet	7 "	... ... "	8	0
China	5 "	... ... "	6	0
Thakuri Kalai	3 "	... ... "	7	0
Arhár	5 "	... ... "	16	8

CULTIVATED AREA.—The District area is given at 3695 square miles, of which 3200 are cultivated. A great difficulty in forming an estimate of the acreage under various crops arises from the difference that exists between various parts of the District as regards the crops chiefly cultivated, a local knowledge of one part not serving for another.

AGRICULTURAL POPULATION.—The Collector has furnished me with no particulars regarding the proportion of agriculturists to labourers. But the Census Report of 1872 (pp. cxviii., cxix.) gives the total "Agricultural and Pastoral Classes" (Hindus) of the Rangpur District at 66,674, including males, females, and children; and exclusive of Musalmáns who live by agriculture, and of the aboriginal and semi-aboriginal castes partly living by cultivation. Analysing the details of population arranged according to occupation at (pp. cxli.–clvii.), I find the total of male adults of class iv.—*i.e.*, persons engaged in agriculture, or with animals—is 547,099. Allowing two other persons as an average of females and children connected with each male adult, the total population living by agriculture, or by taking care of animals, amounts to 1,641,297. Deducting 1153 male adults for the "excepted classes," explained at a foregoing page—*i.e.*, persons possessing estates, or otherwise well off—a balance remains of 545,946 males under class iv.; or, allowing two other persons to each male adult, a total population of 1,637,838 souls living by husbandry, or employed in connection with animals, or tenure-holders belonging to classes who are often people in a small way. The total number of male adult "cultivators" as returned by the Census is 544,494, or, taking the average of two souls to each male adult as family and children, a *net* cultivating population of 1,633,482.

The male adults directly employed in cultivation form about half the total males in the District; and the total number of males, females, and children living by cultivation (allowing two other persons to each male adult), amounts to 1,633,482, or about three-fourths of the total population of the District (2,149,972).

LABOURING POPULATION.—The Census Report of Castes and Nationalities (pp. cxiv.–cxxiii.), returns the labouring classes, below the rank of artisans, of the Rangpur District as follow. Some of the figures have been corrected from the subsequent District Census Statement. The figures do not include Muhammadans:—

1. Aboriginal tribes	1,109
2. Semi-Hinduised aborigines	492,149
3. Personal servant castes	35,595
4. Weaver castes	10,034
5. Labouring castes	212
6. Boating and fishing castes	162,447
7. Musicians and vagabond castes	1,091
8. Unspecified, Vaishnavs, &c.	32,586
Total ...	735,223

Turning to the Statement of Occupation (pp. cxli.–clvii.), I find the following numbers under their respective classes. I only take those who may fairly be considered in the rank of labouring men:—

Class I. (*Government employ*)	Píyádás	420
Class II. (*Professionals*)	Musicians	3,899
Class III. *Service.*	Personal servants ...	16,214
	Sweepers	505
	Water-carriers ...	7
	Unspecified	8,215
Class V. *Conveyance of goods.*	Cartmen	215
	Bullock-drivers ...	122
	Palki-bearers	4,318
	Boatmen	7,743

Class VI. *Poorer sorts of craftsmen.*	Cotton weavers ...	5,475
	Brickmakers	4
	Makers of baskets ...	320
	Shoemakers	61
Class VII. *Miscellaneous.*	Beggars	15,436
	Labourers	29,252
	Unemployed	1,739
	Total ...	93,945

The total population of the District is 2,149,972. Taken by castes, therefore, there are 735,223 persons belonging to labouring classes, or more than one-third of the total population. According to occupation, there are 93,945 male adults, who may fairly be considered in the ranks of labouring men; or 281,835 males, females, and children, comprising over one-eighth of the total population. The discrepancy between the results obtained from the Caste and Occupation Statements, arises from the fact that a large proportion of the aboriginal and semi-aboriginal tribes (who are here entered as labourers) are in reality cultivators. But they form the lowest class of husbandmen, and on the approach of famine, abandon their fields to seek hired labour, and are thus thrown on the labouring population.

The foregoing calculations give, therefore, the following results:—

1. Total population	2,149,972
2. Agriculturists (Hindus) according to caste statement	66,674
3. Agriculturists (total) according to occupation statement	1,637,838
4. Labourers (Hindus and aborigines) according to caste	735,223
5. Labourers (total), according to occupation	281,835
6. Total of Hindu agriculturists and labourers according to caste statement	801,897
7. Total of agriculturists and labourers (all) according to occupation statement ...	1,919,673

N.B.—It should always be remembered that the occupation totals are obtained by multiplying the male adults by three.

MURSHIDABAD DISTRICT.

FAMINE PRICES.—The maximum price of rice during the famine of 1866 was Rs. 6-10 a maund, or 6 seers per rupee, and of paddy Rs. 3-4 per maund. According to the Collector's report of February 1871, prices had not then returned to their ordinary rates before the famine.

FAMINE WARNINGS.—The Collector considers that famine rates should be held to have been reached when ordinary rice sells for 10 or 11 seers per rupee, and at this point he believes Government aid would become necessary. A serious rise of prices, consequent on a partial or total loss of crops, with rates at 15 or 16 seers of rice per rupee in January or February, would be regarded by the Collector as an indication of approaching scarcity, though he would not regard famine as inevitable. If the prospects of the coming harvest continued good, these rates might be maintained throughout the year without any serious harm. The Collector considers the prospects of famine would be very imminent in the event of a total failure of the *aman*, or winter rice crop. If the *aus* harvest had been unusually prolific, actual famine, the Collector thinks, *might* be averted, although he is inclined to doubt it.

MEANS OF TRANSIT.—The means of communication at the disposal of the District are sufficient for the purposes of importation in times of scarcity, and there is no fear of the absolute isolation of any part of this District, except in some portions of the Kándí sub-district, which are extremely difficult of access.

AREA OF THE DISTRICT.—The total area of the District is 1,595,265 acres.

The total of cultivated and cultivable land is given at 1,381,526 acres; waste 213,739, of which long grass and sand cover 58,364 acres. The comparative acreage of the principal crops of the District has not yet been ascertained for the whole area, and differs very widely in the three subdivisions of this District. For the *sadr*, or headquarters subdivision, it may be roughly estimated as follows: of every 10 *bighas*, 4 are under rice; 3 pulse; 2½ wheat and barley; and ½ miscellaneous crops.

In the subdivisions of Kándí and Jangipur the proportion of rice is much greater than four-tenths of the cultivated area.

OUT-TURN OF CROPS.—The yield of paddy varies in different parts of the District. The out-turn rarely bears a fixed relation to the rent of the land, so that it is impossible (as in other Districts) to give definite estimates for land paying rent at Rs. 1-8, and for land at Rs. 3. The Collector accounts for this by stating that there are very few parts of the District where rice-growing lands, paying so high a rate as Rs. 3, are to be met with. In the Lálbágh subdivision not a single *bigha* of rice-producing land probably pays rent at that rate; and within the *sadr*, or headquarters subdivision, the same fact is officially reported. In the second place, the amount of rent paid is not necessarily a criterion of the productive powers of the land, rent depending on various other considerations, among which are the risks of cultivation, especially in the case of failure in the supply of irrigation. Thus land which is highly productive, but liable to frequent disasters, pays less rent than lands less productive but less exposed to mischance. The Collector adduces the instance of the subdivision of Kándí, where rice-lands paying rent at 3 Rs. per *bigha* are less productive than those paying Rs. 1-8. In the Lálbágh subdivision, 8 maunds of paddy per *bigha* is considered to be a fair yield. In the Jangipur subdivision the average yield of one *bigha* of *aus* land is about 6 maunds, and of a *bigha* of *aman* land about 7 maunds. The rate of *aman* land there varies from Re. 1 to Rs. 4. Good *aman* land in a favourable season will yield as much as 11 maunds per *bigha*. In the Kándí subdivision an average out-turn of paddy per *bigha* in Thanas Gokarna and Bharatpur is returned at 10 maunds. In the southern parts of the *sadr* subdivision from 10 to 14 maunds of paddy would be considered a fair yield from a *bigha*, while in the northern tracts the average out-turn is as low as 7 or 8 maunds per *bigha*.

The Journal of the Agricultural Society, 1870, states that the average yield in Murshidábád of a *bigha* of rice-land is 6 or 7 maunds; the maximum 8, and in exceptional places 12 maunds. The value of ordinary paddy is about 12 annas a maund. In addition to the rice crop, a second crop of gram, pulse, peas, or vegetables is sometimes obtained. A crop of peas grown on land which has already borne a rice crop during the year would probably yield 4 or 5 maunds per *bigha*, worth 4 or 5 rupees. A crop of linseed or pulses would differ in quantity, but be about the same value. Represented in maunds, the return of a *bigha* of paddy varies from 6 maunds in the case of inferior land, to 15 maunds in the case of the best kind. Represented in rupees, it may be said to range from Rs. 2-8 in the one case, to Rs. 7-8 in the other; the Collector adds that it is impossible to convey any definite idea of the value of lands which vary so widely.

AGRICULTURAL POPULATION.—The Collector has furnished me with no particulars regarding the proportion of agriculturists to labourers. But the Census Report of 1872 (p. cxviii.) gives the total "Agriculturists and Pastoral Castes" (Hindus) of the Murshidábád District at 199,423, including males, females, and children; exclusive of Musalmáns who live by agriculture, and of the aboriginal and semi-aboriginal castes partly living by cultivation. Analysing the details arranged according to occupation (pp. cxliv., cxlvi.), I find that the total of male adults of class iv., *i.e.*, persons engaged in agriculture or with animals, is 180,804. Allowing two other souls as an average of females and children connected with each male adult, the total population living by agriculture or by taking care of animals amounts to 542,412. Deducting 3388 male adults for the "excepted classes" explained at a foregoing page, *i.e.*, persons possessing estates or otherwise well off, a balance remains of 177,416 males under class iv., or allowing two other persons to each male adult, a total population of 532,248 souls living by husbandry or employed in connection with animals, or tenure-holders belonging to classes who are often people in a small way. This is the *gross* agricultural population. The total number of male adult "cultivators" as returned by the Census is 171,326, or taking the average of two souls to each male adult as family and children, a total population of 513,978. The difference between the results yielded by the Caste and the Occupation Statements is due to the large number of Musalmán cultivators.

The male adults employed in cultivation form about one-fourth of the total males in the District, and the total number of males, females, and children living by cultivation (allowing two other persons to each male) amounts to 513,978, or about two-fifths of the total population of the District (1,353,626).

LABOURING POPULATION.—The Census Report in its statement of Castes and Nationalities (pp. cxiv.–cxxiii.) returns the Hindu labouring classes, below the rank of artisans, of the Murshidábád District as follow. Some of the figures have been corrected from the District Census Statement, subsequently compiled by Mr C. F. Magrath :—

1. Aboriginal tribes ...	... ...	35,318
2. Semi-Hinduised aboriginals	... ...	198,820
3. Personal servant castes	... ...	30,613
4. Weaver castes ...	... ...	24,930
5. Labouring castes ...	... ...	2,866
6. Boating and fishing castes	... ...	26,100
7. Musician and vagabond castes	... ...	671
8. Unspecified, Vaishnavs, &c.	... ...	28,029
	Total ...	347,347

Turning to the Statement of Occupation (pp. cxli.–clvii.), I find the following numbers under their respective classes. I only take those who may fairly be considered in the rank of labouring men:—

Class I. (*Government employ*)	Píyádás ...	41
Class II. (*Professionals*)	Musicians	1,516
Class III. *Service.*	Personal servants ...	2,873
	Sweepers	173
	Water-carriers ...	21
	Unspecified	25,603
Class V. *Conveyance of goods.*	Cartmen	1,724
	Bullock-drivers ...	298
	Palki-bearers ...	2,664
	Boatmen	8,516
Class VI. *Poorer sorts of craftsmen.*	Cotton-weavers ...	11,551
	Basket-makers ...	642
	Cotton-carders ...	23
	Shoe-makers ...	716
	Bird-catcher ...	1
Class VII. *Miscellaneous.*	Beggars	5,903
	Labourers	77,151
	Unemployed ...	4,581
	Total ...	144,003

The total population of the District is 1,353,626. Taken by castes, therefore, there are 347,347 persons belonging to labouring classes, or more than one-fourth of the total population. According to occupation, there are 144,003 male adults who may fairly be considered in the rank of labouring men, or 432,009 males, females, and children, comprising about one-third of the total population.

The foregoing calculations give, therefore, the following net results:—

1. Total population	1,353,626
2. Agriculturists (Hindus) according to caste statement	199,423
3. Agriculturists (total) according to occupation statement	532,248
4. Labourers (Hindus and aborigines) according to caste	347,347
5. Labourers (total) according to occupation ...	432,009
6. Total of Hindu agriculturists and labourers according to caste statement	546,770
7. Total of all agriculturists and labourers according to occupation statement	964,257

N.B.—It should always be remembered that the occupation totals are obtained by multiplying the *male adults* by three.

PABNA DISTRICT.

FAMINE PRICES.—The Collector reported the price of paddy in 1866 at Rs. 2, and that of rice at Rs. 3-14 a maund. In 1871 he wrote to me that prices had not then returned to their ordinary rate previous to the famine. The rates current in 1871 were as follow:—Best cleaned rice, Rs. 1-8-6 per maund; rice used by coolies, Rs. 1-6 per maund; best unshelled paddy, Re. 1 per maund; common unshelled paddy, annas 13 per maund.

FAMINE WARNINGS.—The famine point may be said to be reached when rice sells for over Rs. 4 in January. The means of export and import are so ready at hand that the Collector believes the extremity of famine will never be reached.

The river and the railway would, taken together, avert such a calamity. In Pabna the peasant chiefly depends on the *aman* crop, and a failure of that would inevitably cause a scarcity, but not a famine, unless it was coupled with the loss of the *aus* crop. No Government relief operations were required or undertaken in Pabna District in 1866.

CULTIVATED AREA; OUT-TURN OF CROPS.—The total area of the District is 785,500 acres, and the amount of land under cultivation is 531,542 acres; uncultivated but capable of tillage, 197,391 acres; and jungle and uncultivable, 56,567 acres. The comparative acreage under the principal crops is returned as follows: rice, 425,945 acres; wheat and barley, 17,747 acres; and pulses, 39,931 acres. Most of the land in the District is of the kind commonly known as *dofasli*, yielding two crops, that is, rice and a cold-weather crop of pulses or oil seeds. The produce of a standard *bigha* paying Rs. 1-8 rent would be as follows: *aman* crop, 5 maunds, value Rs. 5; *aus*, 4 maunds, value Rs. 3; spring crop, 1½ maunds, value Rs. 4½, besides straw.

AGRICULTURAL POPULATION.—The Collector has furnished me with no particulars regarding the proportion of agriculturists to labourers. But the Census Report of 1872 (pp. cxviii., cxix.) gives the total "Agricultural and Pastoral Castes" (Hindus) of the Pabna District at 41,225, including males, females, and children; exclusive of Musalmáns who live by agriculture, and of the aboriginal and semi-aboriginal castes partly living by cultivation. By analysing the details of population arranged according to occupation at pp. cxlv., cxlvi., I find that the total male adults of class iv., *i.e.*, persons engaged in agriculture or with animals, is 205,053. Allowing two other persons as an average of females and children connected with each male adult, the total population living by agriculture or in connection with animals amounts to 615,159. Deducting 4169 male adults for the "excepted classes" explained at a foregoing page, *i.e.*, persons possessing estates or otherwise well off, a balance remains of 200,884 males under class iv.; or allowing two other persons to each male adult, a total population of 602,652 souls living by husbandry or employed in connection with animals, or tenure-holders belonging to classes who are often people in a small way. This may be taken as the *gross* agricultural population. The total number of male adult "cultivators" as returned by the Census is 198,731, or taking the average of two persons to each male adult for women and children, a total *net* agricultural population of 596,193.

The male adults employed in cultivation form about one-third of the total males in the District; and the total number of males, females, and children living by cultivation (as obtained by allowing two other persons to each male adult) amounts to 596,193, or less than half of the total population of the District (1,211,594).

LABOURING POPULATION.—The Census Report in its Statement of Castes and Nationalities (pp. cxiv.–cxxii.) returns the labouring classes, below the rank of artisans, of the Pabna District, as follow, exclusive of Musalmáns :—

1. Aborigines	503
2. Semi-Hinduised aborigines	80,446
3. Personal servant castes	14,490
4. Weaver castes	12,741
5. Labouring castes	5,362
6. Boating and fishing castes	50,519
7. Beggar and vagabond castes	346
8. Unspecified, Vaishnavs, &c.	23,676
Total ...	188,083

Turning to the Statement of Occupation (pp. cxli.–clvii.), I find the following numbers under the respective classes. I only take those who may fairly be considered in the rank of labouring men :—

Class	Occupation	MALE ADULTS.
Class I. (*Government employ*)	Píyádás ...	12
Class II. (*Professionals*)	Musicians ...	1,414
Class III. *Service.*	Personal servants	8,538
	Sweepers	276
	Water-carriers ...	1
	Unspecified ...	9,417
Class V. *Conveyance of goods.*	Cartmen	362
	Bullock-drivers ...	94
	Palki-bearers ...	2,696
	Boatmen	11,906
Class VI. *Poorer sorts of craftsmen.*	Well-diggers ...	38
	Basket-makers ...	228
	Cotton-weavers ...	15,684
	Cotton-carders ...	5
	Cotton-spinners ...	22
	Shoe-makers ...	280

Class VII. *Miscellaneous.*	Beggars	4,832
	Labourers ...	30,288
	Unemployed ...	3,621
	Total ...	89,714

The total population of the District is 1,211,594. Taken by castes, therefore, there are 188,083 persons belonging to labouring classes, or nearly one-seventh of the total population. According to occupation, there are 89,714 male adults, or allowing two other persons to each adult as family, a total of 269,142 males, females, and children, being more than one-fifth of the total population. The discrepancy between the results obtained from the Caste and Occupation Statements is owing to the Musalmán labourers being not included in the former.

The foregoing calculations give the following results:—

1. Total population	1,211,594
2. Agriculturists (Hindus) according to caste statement	41,225
3. Agriculturists (total) according to occupation statement	602,652
4. Labouring population according to caste statement (Hindus, aborigines, &c.) ...	188,083
5. Labouring population (total) according to occupation	269,142
6. Total (Hindu) agriculturists and labourers according to caste statement	229,308
7. Total of all agriculturists and labourers according to occupation statement	871,794

N.B.—It must be remembered that the total of agriculturists and labourers, according to occupation, is obtained by multiplying the number of *male adults* by three.

BOGRA DISTRICT.

FAMINE PRICES.—The Collector, in his report dated April 1871, states that in 1866 coarse cleaned rice rose to Rs. 4 per maund, and fine cleaned rice to Rs. 6. He reported that local prices had then (1871) fallen to their ordinary standard before the famine. No death from actual starvation was reported during the famine, but the Collector thinks that the ordinary mortality was increased by disease brought on by insufficiency of food. It was said that in some households men and children lived on half rations, and women on rice-water and roots. If, therefore, the rates quoted had long continued, relief would probably have been necessary.

FAMINE WARNINGS.—Warnings of famine are—(1.) Total want of rain in September and October; (2.) loss of the *aman* crop from this or any other cause; and (3.) prices; thus if common rice reached Rs. 3 per maund after the *aman* harvest. The Collector, however, remarks that prices later in the year depend as much on the prospects of the growing crops as on the out-turn of the past harvest. He quotes the previous year (1870) as an instance, when rice stood at Rs. 1-5 per maund in January, and fell before the next harvest to Re. 1 per maund.

CULTIVATED AREA; OUT-TURN OF CROPS.—This District depends on the *aman* crops. The *aus* crop, it is stated, grows on too small a scale to compensate for the failure of the *aman*.

ORDINARY OUT-TURN.—Three-fourths of the cultivated land are under rice. The quantity of barley, peas, and Indian-corn grown is insignificant. The average rent of paddy land falls below Rs. 1-4; very little land is found at so high a rent as Rs. 3 per *bigha*.

A *bigha* at Rs. 1-8 produces on an average about 12 maunds of paddy, value Rs. 6, besides straw. A second crop of peas is sometimes sown, when the Bona rice is half grown, and may yield 2 maunds per *bigha*, value Rs. 2.

MEANS OF TRANSIT.—With the railway to Goálanda, the Daokoba river open to steamers all the year round, the Karatoya and minor channels in various parts of the District navigable during the rains, and fair roads connecting Bogra with Sirajganj and Nator in dry weather, the Collector does not think importation would be difficult. The Collector does not lay any stress on the communication between Bogra and Rangpur or Bogra and

Dinájpur, because in the event of a severe famine they would probably suffer equally with his own District.

AGRICULTURAL POPULATION.—The Collector has given me no information either as to the famine of 1866, or as to what prices may be considered as famine rates, or as to the proportion of the agricultural to the labouring population. On this latter point the Census Report of 1872 (pp. cxviii., cxix.) returns the total "Agricultural and Pastoral Castes" (Hindus) of the Bogra District at 23,776, including males, females, and children; but exclusive of Musalmáns who follow agriculture, and aboriginal or semi-aboriginal tribes partly living by cultivation. The Musalmáns, however, comprise 80 per cent. of the total population of the District, and the above estimate of cultivators from the Caste Statement is, therefore, not even approximate to the real number of the inhabitants employed in tillage.

By analysing the details of population arranged according to occupation (pp. cxliv.–cxlvi.), I find that the total male adults of class iv. *i.e.*, persons engaged in agriculture or in tending animals, is 170,057. Allowing two other persons as an average of females and children connected with each male adult, the total population living by agriculture or in connection with animals amounts to Rs. 510,171. Deducting 959 male adults for the "excepted classes" explained at a foregoing page, *i.e.*, persons possessing estates or otherwise well off, a balance remains of 169,098 males under class iv.; or allowing two other persons to each male adult, a total population of 507,294 souls living by husbandry or employed in connection with animals, or tenure-holders belonging to classes who are often men in a small way. This may be taken as the *gross* agricultural population. The total number of male adult "cultivators" as returned by the Census is 168,742, or taking the average of two persons to each male adult for women and children, a total *net* "agricultural" population of 506,226.

The male adults employed in agri culture form about half the males in the District, and the total number of males, females, and children living by cultivation (as obtained by allowing two other persons to each male adult) amounts to 506,226, or about five-sevenths of the total population of the District (689,467).

LABOURING POPULATION.—The Census Report in its Statement of Castes and Nationalities (pp. cxiv.–cxxv.) returns the labouring classes, below the rank of artisans, of the Bogra District, as follows. Some of the figures have been corrected from the District Census Statement compiled by Mr C. F. Magrath :—

1. Aborigines	318
2. Semi-Hinduised aborigines	38,339
3. Personal servant castes	4,979
4. Weaver castes	7,151
5. Labouring castes	3,060
6. Boating and fishing castes	15,807
7. Beggar and vagabond castes	48
8. Unspecified, Vaishnavs, &c.	9,067
Total ...	78,769

Turning to the Statement of Occupations (pp. cxli.-clvii.), I find the following numbers under their respective classes. I only take those who may fairly be considered in the rank of labouring men :—

Class	Occupation	MALE ADULTS.
Class II. (*Professionals*)	Musicians	1,540
Class III. *Service.*	Personal servants ...	2,777
	Sweepers	15
	Water-carriers	2
	Unspecified	3,580
Class V. *Conveyance of goods.*	Cartmen	7
	Palki-bearers	827
	Boatmen	504
Class VI. *Poorer craftsmen.*	Cotton-weavers ...	3,115
	Basket-makers	78
	Cotton-spinners ...	6
	Shoe-makers	2
Class VII. *Miscellaneous.*	Beggars	4,006
	Labourers	6,057
	Unemployed	424
	Total ...	22,940

The total population of the District is 689,467. Taken by castes, therefore, there are 78,769 persons belonging to labouring classes, or about one-ninth of the total population. According to occupation, there are 22,940 male adults, or allowing two other persons to each male adult as family, a total of 68,820 males, females, and children, being about one-tenth of the total population. The discrepancy between the results obtained from the Occupation and Caste Statements is probably owing to a number of semi-Hinduised aboriginals (who are here entered as labourers) living by cultivation or fishing.

The foregoing calculations yield the following results:—

1. Total population	689,467
2. Hindu agriculturists according to caste statement	23,776
3. Agriculturists (total) according to occupation statement	507,294
4. Labouring population (Hindus, &c.) according to caste statement	78,769
5. Labouring population (total) according to occupation	68,820
6. Hindu agriculturists and labourers according to caste statement	102,545
7. Total of all agriculturists and labourers according to occupation statement	576,114

N.B.—It must be remembered that the total of agriculturists and labourers, according to occupation, is obtained by multiplying the number of *male adults* by three.

DINAJPUR DISTRICT.

FAMINE PRICES.—The Collector states to me, in his report, January 1871, that the maximum prices of rice during the famine were as follows:—Best cleaned rice, Rs. 4-7 per maund; common rice, Rs. 4-1-6 per maund. Local prices, at date of report, had returned to their ordinary rates before the famine.

FAMINE WARNINGS.—The *aman* or winter rice is the principal crop of Dinàjpur, and if it failed, the *aus* would not suffice to feed the people; fortunately, however, he states that the *aman* harvest has never been known to fail altogether. The Collector is of opinion that importation will never be necessary unless some very great and unforeseen change takes place in the country.

OUT-TURN OF CROPS, AND AREA OF CULTIVATION.—The total area of the District is 3,311,658 acres, and the estimated cultivated area 2,032,287 acres. Of the remaining 1,279,371 acres of uncultivated, about 852,914 are incapable of cultivation. The comparative acreage under rice is roughly estimated at 1,016,148 acres. Barley and Indian corn are also grown in Dinájpur, but no evidence exists showing the area under these crops.

A good average yield from land paying Rs. 1-8 per *bigha* would be from 8 to 10 maunds of paddy, value from Rs. 5 to Rs. 7. Land paying Rs. 3 yields 16 or 17 maunds of paddy, worth from Rs. 10 to Rs. 12. Upon some lands a second crop of pulse or oil seed is grown, the average value of the produce being from Rs. 5 to Rs. 7 per *bigha*. *Khayer* land (a black soil), letting at from 2 annas to Rs. 2 per *bigha*, produces only one rice crop in the year, but *Poli* land, letting at from Rs. 1 to Rs. 3-8, produces a cold-weather crop besides. It is impossible to estimate the value of these cold-weather crops, owing to their variety and different prices. Perhaps an average of Rs. 5 to Rs. 7 per *bigha* might be accepted as a fair value of their out-turn. The Collector considers that a good return from land yielding both crops, and paying a rental of Rs. 1-8 a *bigha*, would be 9½ to 12 maunds of produce, valued at Rs. 9 to Rs. 13; and from land at Rs. 3 per *bigha*, 18 to 20 maunds, valued at Rs. 15 to Rs. 19.

AGRICULTURAL POPULATION.—The Collector has furnished me with no particulars regarding the proportion of agriculturists to labourers. The Census Report of 1872 (pp. cxviii., cxix.) returns the total "Agricultural and Pastoral Castes" (Hindus) of the Dinájpur District at 50,813, including males, females, and children; but exclusive of Musalmáns who live by agriculture, and of the aboriginal and semi-aboriginal castes partly living by cultivation. But by analysing the details of population arranged according to occupation at pp. cxliv.–cxlvi., I find that the total male adults under class iv., *i.e.*, persons engaged in agriculture or with animals, is 362,352. Allowing two other souls as an average of females and children connected with each male adult, the total population living by agriculture or in connection with animals amounts to 1,087,056. Deducting 1117 male adults for the "excepted classes" explained at a foregoing page, *i.e.*, persons possessing estates or otherwise well off, a balance remains of 361,235 males under class iv.; or allowing two other persons to each male adult, a total population of 1,083,705 persons living by husbandry or employed in connection with animals, or tenure-holders belonging to classes who are often people in a small way. This is the *gross* agricultural population. The total number of male adult "cultivators" as returned by the Census is 351,632, or taking the average of two souls to each male adult as family and children, a total *net* agricultural population of 1,054,896. The Musalmáns form 52 p.c. of the inhabitants.

The male adults directly employed in cultivation form about three-sevenths of the total males in the District; and the total males, females, and children living by cultivation number 1,054,896, or nearly five-sevenths of the total population of the District (1,501,924).

LABOURING POPULATION.—The Census Report in its Statement of Castes and Nationalities (pp. cxiv.–cxxv.) returns the labouring classes, below the rank of artisans, of the Dinájpur District, as follows. Some of the figures have been corrected from the District Census Statement subsequently compiled by Mr C. F. Magrath :—

1. Aborigines	4,431
2. Semi-Hinduised aborigines	505,527
3. Personal servant castes	20,498
4. Weaver castes	23,969
5. Labouring castes	550
6. Boating and fishing castes	31,206
7. Musician and vagabond castes	619
8. Unspecified, Vaishnavs, &c.	26,963
Total ...	613,763

Turning to the Statement of Occupation (pp. cxli.–clvii.), I find the following numbers under their respective classes. I only take those who may fairly be considered in the rank of labouring men :—

Class II. (*Professionals*)	Musicians	1,940
Class III. *Service.*	Personal servants ...	1,233
	Sweepers	278
	Water-carriers	2
	Unspecified	23,449

Class V. *Conveyance of goods.*	Cartmen	1,030
	Bullock-drivers	4
	Palki-bearers	1,195
	Boatmen	2,587
Class VI. *Poorer sorts of craftsmen.*	Lime-burners	33
	Cotton-weavers	4,001
	Basket-makers	226
	Cotton-carders	10
	Cotton-spinners	65
	Shoe-makers	125
Class VII. *Miscellaneous.*	Beggars	7,046
	Labourers	37,525
	Unemployed	1,692
	Total	82,441

The total population of the District is 1,501,924. Taken by castes, therefore, there are 613,763 persons belonging to the labouring classes, or about two-fifths of the total population. According to occupation, there are 82,441 male adults who may fairly be considered in the rank of labouring men, or 247,323 males, females, and children, comprising over one-seventh of the total population. The discrepancy between the results obtained from the Caste and Occupation Statements arises from the fact that a large proportion of the aboriginal and semi-aboriginal tribes (who are here entered as labourers) are in reality cultivators. But they form the lowest class of husbandmen, and on the approach of famine abandon their fields to seek hired labour, and are thus thrown on the labouring population.

1. Total population	1,501,924
2. Agriculturists (Hindus) according to caste statement	50,813
3. Agriculturists (total) according to occupation statement	1,083,705
4. Labourers (Hindus and aborigines) according to caste statement	613,763
5. Labourers (total) according to occupation statement	247,323
6. Total (Hindus) agriculturists and labourers according to caste statement	664,576

7. Total of all agriculturists and labourers according to occupation statement ... 1,331,028

N.B.—It must be remembered that the total of agriculturists and labourers, according to occupation, is obtained by multiplying the number of male adults by three.

MALDAH DISTRICT.

FAMINE PRICES.—The Collector in his report to me, dated February 1871, states that during the famine of 1866 the price of rice rose to 10 seers a rupee, or 4 rupees a maund; and that of paddy to 18 seers a rupee, or Rs. 2-4 per maund. These prices, however, did not continue long; nor did they even reach a point which necessitated relief from Government. In 1871 prices had not returned to what they were before the famine. Rice at 10 seers per rupee and a corresponding increase in the prices of other edible grains are considered by the Collector to amount to famine rates. Any rates higher than these would, the Collector thinks, require Government interference in order to ward off starvation.

FAMINE WARNINGS.—The Collector considers a serious failure of the *aman* crop, coupled with great rise in prices in January and February, as sure precursors of a famine. The District mainly depends on the *aman* or winter rice crop; the *aus* or autumn crop could not make up for the total loss of the former, or enable the people to live through the year without actual famine.

CULTIVATED AREA.—The total area of the District is returned at 824,521 acres, of which 426,583 are cultivated, 244,130 cultivable, and 153,808 uncultivable. I have received the following estimate of the comparative acreage under the principal crops:—Rice, 250,000 acres; wheat, 25,000 acres; other food-grains, 10,000 acres.

OUT-TURN OF CROPS.—The Collector returns from 10 to 12 maunds of paddy per *bigha* as a fair yield for land renting from Rs. 1-4 to Rs. 1-8, and from 7 to 10 maunds for inferior lands. No rice-land in Maldah District rents higher than Rs. 1-8 a *bigha.* The value of the out-turn from such land varies from Rs. 15 to Rs. 18 a *bigha*, and from inferior land Rs. 10 to Rs. 15 a *bigha.* The winter crop of pulses and oil seeds yields from 5 to 7 maunds a *bigha*, value Rs. 7 to Rs. 10. A fair return of both rice and winter crops would be from 16 to 20 maunds of produce, value from Rs. 20 to Rs. 25.

Agricultural Population.—The Collector has furnished me with no particulars regarding the proportion of agriculturists to labourers. The Census Report of 1872 (pp. cxviii., cxix.) returns the total "Agricultural and Pastoral Castes" (Hindus) of the Maldah District at 64,273, including males, females, and children; but exclusive of Musalmáns who live by agriculture, and of the aboriginal and semi-aboriginal castes living by cultivation. But by analysing the details of population arranged according to occupation at pp. cxliv.–cxlvi., I find that the total of male adults of class iv., *i.e.*, persons engaged in agriculture or with animals, is 102,710. Allowing two other persons as an average of females and children connected with each male adult, the total population living by agriculture or in connection with animals amounts to 308,130. Deducting 916 male adults for the "excepted classes" explained at a foregoing page, *i.e.*, persons possessing estates or otherwise well off, a balance remains of 101,794 males under class iv.; or allowing two other persons to each male adult, a total population of 305,382 souls living by husbandry or employed in connection with animals, or tenure-holders belonging to classes who are often people in a small way. This is the *gross* agricultural population. The total number of male adult "cultivators" as returned by the Census is 99,213, or taking the average of two persons to each male adult for women and children, a total *net* agricultural population of 297,639.

The male adults directly employed in cultivation form three-tenths of the total males in the District; and the total number of males, females, and children living by cultivation amounts to 297,639, or about three-sevenths of the total population of the District (676,426).

Labouring Population.—The Census Report in its Statement of Castes and Nationalities (pp. cxiv.–cxxv.) returns the labouring classes, below the rank of artisans, of the Maldah District, as follows. I have verified the figures from the subsequent District Census Statements compiled by Mr C. F. Margrath:—

1.	Aborigines	11,717
2.	Semi-Hinduised aboriginals	135,562
3.	Personal-servant castes	21,616
4.	Weaver castes	18,412
5.	Labouring castes	1,304
6.	Boating and fishing castes	24,476
7.	Musician and vagabond castes	136
8.	Unspecified, Vaishnavs, &c.	17,578
	Total	230,801

Turning to the Statement of Occupations (pp. cxli.–clvii.), I find the following numbers under their respective classes. I only take those who may fairly be considered in the rank of labouring men :—

Class	Occupation	MALE ADULTS.
Class I. (*Government Employ*)	Píyádás	11
Class II. (*Professionals*)	Musicians	492
Class III. *Service.*	Personal servants	7,565
	Sweepers	72
	Water-carriers	17
	Unspecified	3,329
Class V. *Conveyance of goods.*	Cartmen	326
	Bullock-drivers	420
	Palkí-bearers	579
	Boatmen	9,631
Class VI. *Poorer sorts of craftsmen.*	Brick-makers	2
	Cage-makers	297
	Basket-makers	18
	Cotton-carders	143
	Cotton-spinners	142
	Cotton-weavers	4,654
	Shoe-makers	872
Class VII. *Miscellaneous.*	Beggars	2,310
	Labourers	28,933
	Unemployed	2,207
	Total	62,020

The total population of the District is 676,426. Taken by castes, therefore, there are 230,801 Hindus belonging to labouring classes, or about one-third of the total population. According to occupation, there are 62,020 male adults who may fairly be considered in the rank of labouring men, or 186,060 males, females and children, being about two-sevenths of the total population. The discrepancies between the results obtained from the Caste and Occupation Statements arise from the fact that a large proportion of the aboriginal and semi-aboriginal tribes (who are here entered as labourers) are in reality cultivators. But they form the lowest class of husbandmen, and on the approach of famine abandon their fields to seek hired labour, and are thus thrown on the labouring population. The Musalmáns form 46 per cent.

The foregoing calculations yield the following results :—

1. Total population	676,426
2. Agriculturists (Hindus) according to caste statement	64,273
3. Agriculturists (total) according to occupation statement	305,382
4. Labourers (Hindus) according to caste statement	230,801
5. Labouring population (total) according to occupation	186,060
6. Total Hindu agriculturists and labourers, according to caste statement	295,074
7. Total of all agriculturists and labourers according to occupation statement	491,442

N.B.—It must be remembered that the total of agriculturists and labourers, according to occupation, is obtained by multiplying the number of male *adults* by three.

BARDWAN DIVISION.

BARDWAN DISTRICT.

Famine Prices.—During the twelve months of 1866 the following prices obtained for coarse rice, as returned in the report of the Famine Commissioners (printed 1867):—January, $12\frac{5}{16}$ seers per rupee; February, $11\frac{1}{4}$ seers per rupee; March, $10\frac{7}{8}$ seers per rupee; April, $10\frac{7}{8}$ seers per rupee; May, $10\frac{1}{15}$ seers per rupee; June, $9\frac{7}{16}$ seers per rupee; July, $8\frac{3}{8}$ seers per rupee; August, $7\frac{9}{16}$ seers per rupee; September, $8\frac{3}{8}$ seers per rupee; October, $8\frac{5}{16}$ seers per rupee; November, $8\frac{5}{8}$ seers per rupee; December, $18\frac{1}{4}$ seers per rupee. The Collector, in his report dated July 1871, states that in 1870 ordinary rice sold for Rs. 1-10 per maund, and that prices had nearly gone down to the ordinary rates.

Famine Warnings.—Relief operations in 1866 became necessary when the price of rice had risen to 7 or 8 seers per rupee. The Collector is of opinion that famine is to be apprehended when two crops have failed successively, followed by a general drought. He would accept it to be a warning of famine if rice rises to 16 seers per rupee in the month of January. The District depends almost entirely upon the *aman* or winter crop for its food supply, and a failure of this could not, in the opinion of the Collector, be compensated by the *aus* or autumn rice crop, which is grown on a comparatively small scale.

Means of Transit.—The facilities for communication are, on the whole, deemed sufficient to contend with the extremity of famine in the greater part of the District; but there are certain parts where the communication is very imperfect, and which are difficult of approach, especially during the rains.

Cultivated Area.—The total area of the District is 3158

square miles. No trustworthy statistics exist as to the amount of land under cultivation, but a rough estimate by the Collector gives 2697 square miles as the cultivated area.

OUT-TURN OF CROPS.—A fair yield of paddy per *bigha* from land paying rent at Rs. 3 is from 10 to 16 maunds, valued at from Rs. 5 to 10; and from land paying a rental of Rs. 1-8, 5 to 8 maunds of paddy, value Rs. 5 to 8. In some instances two crops, consisting of *aman* rice followed by *khesari*, are raised on the same land; this, however, is exceptionable. The annual profit of one *bigha* paying a rent of Rs. 3 is returned at about Rs. 6, and half that amount may be taken as the profit from a *bigha* of land rented at Rs. 1-8.

The following brief particulars of the effect of the famine of 1866 in Bardwán are reproduced in a condensed form from the District narrative in the Report of the Famine Commissioners:

HISTORY OF THE FAMINE OF 1866.—The early *aus* crop of 1865 was good; the *aman* throughout the District did not probably average less than two-thirds of a full out-turn. By March 1866, however, coarse rice, which ordinarily sells from Rs. 1-4 to Rs. 2 per maund at that time of the year, was realising Rs. 4-8 a maund. In June the price was Rs. 5, against Rs. 2-2 a maund, the usual rate in that month. On the 11th of July a meeting of gentlemen was held to consider the state of affairs. Subscriptions were raised, and on the 15th July a relief-house was opened at which cooked food was distributed. The number of applicants for relief rose rapidly, and on the 27th the Committee applied to the Commissioner for assistance from Government.

On the 23d July the Mahárájá opened a special *annachhatra*, or feeding-house for the paupers. The daily attendance at first was 1200. On the 17th August the Commissioner applied for, and on the 27th the Board of Revenue granted, a sum of Rs. 3000 for relief purposes, followed shortly afterwards by a grant of Rs. 2000 from the Calcutta Relief Committee. On receipt of these funds, the Commissioner, under instructions from the Board, caused a local committee to be formed, consisting of officials as well as of private gentlemen. The Commissioner also urged the adoption of a system under which those who were capable of light labour should be employed. At the first meeting of the Committee, an offer was made by the Mahárájá of Bardwán to provide for all the destitute paupers in Bardwán town at his own expense, the arrangements being subject to the supervision and approval of the Commissioner. This munificent offer was at once accepted, and from the 6th of September the work of gratuitous relief was made over to the Mahárájá. The total expenditure incurred by the Mahárájá up to 4th November, when gratuitous relief ceased, was Rs. 14,550.

GENERAL REVIEW.—"Speaking comparatively, the people of the District did not suffer severely. The generally prosperous condition of the land-holding peasants, caused by their proximity to the Calcutta markets, enabled them to oppose a greater power of resistance to famine than that which could be offered by the peasants in less advanced Districts to the west and south-west. They also received much support from their landlords.

"The day labourers were driven into the towns to seek a subsistence, and swelled the crowds of paupers who had come in from Districts which had suffered more severely. In these centres, death and disease were unavoidable. Although the external relief granted to this District was small, we think that it did not probably fall short of the requirements. It would, however, have been well if the organised relief at the different points in the interior of the District had begun earlier in the season." (Famine Commissioners' Report.)

The total amount placed at the disposal of the District Relief Committee is returned by the Famine Commissioners as under:

Granted by the Board of Revenue, Rs. 3000; by the Calcutta Relief Committee, Rs. 2000; local private subscriptions, Rs. 3005; total, Rs. 8005. This is exclusive of the expenditure incurred by the Mahárájá (Rs. 14,550).

AGRICULTURAL POPULATION.—The Collector of the District does not furnish any particulars regarding the proportion of agriculturists to labourers. But the Census Report of 1872 (p. cxviii.) gives the total "Agricultural and Pastoral Castes" of the Bardwán District at 433,758, including males, females, and children, exclusive of Musalmáns living by agriculture. By analysing the details of population arranged according to occupation at pp. cxlv., cxlvi., I find that the total male adults of class iv., *i.e.*, persons engaged in agriculture or in tending animals, amount to 337,249. Allowing two other persons as an average for women and children connected with each male adult, the total population living by agriculture or by tending animals amounts to 1,011,747. Deducting 12,508 male adults for the "excepted classes" explained at a foregoing page, *i.e.*, persons possessing estates or otherwise well off, a balance remains of 324,741 males under class iv.; or allowing two persons to each male adult, a total population of 974,223 souls living by husbandry or employed in connection with animals, or tenure-holders belonging to classes who are often people in a small way. This may be taken as the *gross* agricultural population. The total number of male adult "cultivators" as returned by the Census is 315,477, or taking the average of two persons to each male adult as family and children, a total *net* cultivating population of 946,431.

The male adults employed in tillage form about one-third of the total males in the District; and the total number of males, females, and children living by cultivation (as obtained by allowing two other persons to each male adult) amounts to 946,431, or about half the total population of the District (2,034,745).

LABOURING POPULATION.—The Census Report in its Statement of Castes and Nationalities (pp. cxiv.–cxxiv.) returns the labouring classes, below the rank of artisans, of the Bardwán District, as follow :—

1. Aborigines	8,103
2. Semi-Hinduised aborigines	454,184
3. Personal servant castes	58,898
4. Weaver castes	56,138
5. Labouring castes	2,566
6. Boating and fishing castes	25,475
7. Beggar and vagabond castes	3,084
8. Unspecified, Vaishnavs, &c.	80,617
Total ...	689,065

Turning to the Statement of Occupations (pp. cxli.–clvii.), I find the following numbers under their respective classes. I only take those who may fairly be considered in the ranks of labouring men :—

		MALE ADULTS.
Class I. (*Government employ*)	Piyádás ...	261
Class II. (*Professionals*)	Musicians	2,683
Class III. *Service.*	Personal servants ...	8,688
	Sweepers	180
	Water-carriers ...	65
	Unspecified ...	20,099

Class V. *Conveyance of goods, &c.*	Cartmen	1,633
	Bullock-drivers ...	322
	Palki-bearers ...	6,329
	Boatmen	2,495
Class VI. *Poorer craftsmen.*	Lime-burners ...	230
	Basket-makers ...	1,959
	Weavers in cotton ...	24,557
	Shoe-makers ...	1,322
Class VII. *Miscellaneous.*	Beggars	14,033
	Labourers	102,197
	Unemployed ...	14,560
	Total ...	201,613

The total population of the District is 2,034,745. Taken by castes, therefore, there are 689,065 persons belonging to the labouring classes, or one-third of the total population. According to occupation, there are 201,613 male adults, or allowing two other persons to each male adult as family and children, a total of 604,839 males, females, and children, or three-tenths of the total population of the District. Bardwán is purely an agricultural District, and almost every family, from the highest Bráhman to the lowest *Hárí*, possesses land, and at least partly lives by agriculture. The discrepancy between the results obtained from Caste and Occupation Statements is probably owing to a great proportion of the low castes entered above as labourers living by cultivation; but here, as elsewhere, they form the lowest class of husbandmen, and on the approach of famine abandon their fields to seek hired labour, and are thus thrown on the labouring population. There are also many Musalmán cultivators.

The foregoing calculations yield the following net results:—

1. Total population	2,034,745
2. Agriculturists according to caste statement (Hindus)	433,758
3. Agriculturists (all) according to occupation statement	974,223
4. Labourers according to caste statement (Hindus)	689,065
5. Labourers (all) according to occupation ...	604,839

6. Total agriculturists and labourers (Hindus) according to caste statement 1,122,823
7. Total agriculturists and labourers (all) according to occupation statement ... 1,579,062

It must be remembered that the total of agriculturists and labourers according to occupation is obtained by multiplying the *male adults* by three.

BIRBHUM DISTRICT.

FAMINE PRICES.—The Collector, in his report dated February 1871, states that the maximum prices during the famine of 1866 were 8 seers of rice and 16 seers of paddy per rupee. In 1871 the Collector wrote to me that prices had returned to what were considered ordinary rates previous to the famine. The current rates then were—for best cleaned rice, Rs. 2-10 per maund; coarse rice, Rs. 1-4 per maund; best paddy, Rs. 1-5 per maund; common paddy, 10 annas per maund.

FAMINE WARNINGS.—The Collector would consider that if rice sells at 12 seers per rupee, it would be a famine rate. The District depends chiefly on the *aman* or winter harvest, and the Collector reports that in case of its failure, the *aus* or autumn crop could not be depended on as a substitute.

MEANS OF TRANSIT.—The means at the disposal of the District are, in the opinion of the Collector, amply sufficient to avert the extremity of famine by importation from other parts. These consist of the railway, rivers, and channels; and the Collector states that they afford sufficient facilities for importation, as to prevent danger of isolation of any particular part of the District in time of famine. The Collector offers no suggestions regarding remedial or mitigating measures during famines.

CULTIVATED AREA; OUT-TURN OF CROPS.—A fair out-turn from a *bigha* of land paying a rent of Rs. 1-8 is returned by the Collector at from 6 to 8 maunds of paddy. Very little land rents as high as Rs. 3 per *bigha*, but the Collector states that such land ought to yield an out-turn of from 12 to 16 maunds of paddy. Land paying this rate ordinarily produces 10 maunds of paddy, besides a second or cold-weather crop, consisting of, say, 3 maunds of wheat. The total value of the produce of such land would be from Rs. 12 to 15 per *bigha*. An average value of the yield of the poorer descriptions of land is estimated by the Collector at from Rs. 5 to Rs. 7 per *bigha*.

The area of the District is returned by the Collector at 1,278,171 acres, of which 871,846 acres were under cultivation. As a rough estimate, the Collector considers that about 15-16ths of the total cultivated area are under rice.

AGRICULTURAL POPULATION.—The Collector has furnished me with no particulars regarding the proportion of agriculturists to labourers. But the Census Report of 1872 (pp. cxviii., cxix.), returns the total "Agricultural and Pastoral Castes" (Hindus) of the Bírbhúm District at 148,766, including males, females, and children; exclusive of Musalmáns who live by agriculture, and of the aboriginal and semi-aboriginal castes partly living by cultivation. But by analysing the details of population arranged according to occupation at pp. cxliv.–cxlvi., I find that the total male adults of class iv., *i.e.*, persons engaged in agriculture or with animals, is 119,844. Allowing two other persons as an average for females and children connected with each male adult, the total population living by agriculture or in connection with animals amounts to 359,532. Deducting 1694 male adults for the "excepted classes" explained at a foregoing page, *i.e.*, persons possessing estates or otherwise well off, a balance remains of 118,150 males under class iv.; or allowing two other persons to each male adult, a total population of 354,450 souls living by husbandry or employed in connection with animals, or tenure-holders belonging to classes who are often people in a small way. This may be taken as the *gross* agricultural population. The total number of male adult "cultivators" as returned by the Census is 115,280; or taking the average of two persons to each male adult as family and children, a *net* cultivating population of 345,840.

The male adults employed in cultivation form nearly one-third of the total males in the District; and the total number of males, females, and children living by cultivation (as estimated by allowing two other persons to each male adult) amounts to 345,840, or about one-half of the total population of the District (696,945).

LABOURING POPULATION.—The Census Report, in its Statement of Castes and Nationalities (pp. cxiv.–cxxiii.) returns the labouring classes, below the rank of artisans, for the Bírbhúm District, as follow. The figures have been corrected from the subsequent District Census Statements by Mr C. F. Magrath:—

1. Aboriginal	16,276
2. Semi-Hinduised aborigines	181,147
3. Personal servant castes	12,555
4. Weaver castes	20,621
5. Labouring castes	4,520
6. Boating and fishing castes	2,966
7. Musician and vagabond castes	559
8. Unspecified, Vaishnavs, &c.	25,869
Total ...	264,513

Turning to the Statement of Occupation (pp. cxli.-clvii.), I find the following numbers under their respective classes. I only take those who may fairly be considered in the rank of labouring men:—

		MALE ADULTS.
Class I. (*Government employ*)	Píyádás	23
Class II. (*Professionals*)	Musicians ...	1,038
Class III. *Service.*	Personal servants	4,673
	Sweepers ...	69
	Water-carriers ...	6
	Unspecified ...	97
Class V. *Conveyance of goods.*	Cartmen ...	567
	Bullock-drivers ...	195
	Palki-bearers ...	1,472
	Boatmen ...	8
Class VI. *Poorer sorts of craftsmen.*	Brick-makers ...	1
	Well-diggers ...	1
	Basket-makers ...	712
	Cotton-carders ...	4
	Cotton-spinners ...	2
	Cotton-weavers ...	7,531
	Shoe-makers ...	918
Class VII. *Miscellaneous.*	Beggars	4,312
	Labourers ...	36,138
	Unemployed ...	1,738
	Total ...	59,775

The total population of the District is 696,945. Taken by castes, therefore, there are 264,513 persons belonging to the labouring classes, or about three-eighths of the total population. According to occupation, there are 59,775 male adults, or 179,325 males, females, and children, comprising over one-fourth of the total population. The discrepancy between the figures obtained for the labourers from the Caste and Occupation Statements, probably arises from the fact that a large proportion of the aboriginal and semi-aboriginal tribes (who are here entered as labourers) are in reality cultivators. But they form the lowest class of husbandmen, and on the approach of famine abandon their fields to seek hired labour, and are thus thrown on the labouring population.

The foregoing calculations give the following results :—

1. Total population	696,954
2. Agriculturists (Hindus) according to caste statement	148,766
3. Agriculturists (all) according to occupation statement	354,450
4. Labouring population according to caste (Hindus, aborigines, and semi-aborigines)	264,513
5. Labouring population (all) according to occupation statement	179,325
6. Total agriculturists and labourers according to caste statement (Hindus, &c.) ...	413,279
7. Total agriculturists and labourers according to occupation statement	533,775

N.B.—It must be remembered that the total of agriculturists and labourers, according to occupation, is obtained by multiplying the number of male adults by three.

BANKURA DISTRICT.

FAMINE PRICES.—The following were the price rates of ordinary rice during each month of the famine year of 1866, as returned by the Famine Commissioners :—January, 15 seers per rupee ;

February, 13 seers per rupee; March, $12\frac{1}{2}$ seers per rupee; April, $11\frac{7}{8}$ seers per rupee; May, 10 seers per rupee; June, $7\frac{1}{2}$ seers per rupee; July, $6\frac{9}{16}$ per rupee; August, 6 seers per rupee; September, $5\frac{1}{2}$ seers per rupee; October, $15\frac{1}{4}$ seers per rupee; November, 17 seers per rupee; December, 17 seers per rupee. The Collector in his report to me, dated March 1871, stated that prices had not then returned to their ordinary rates previous to the famine. In his opinion, Government relief operations become necessary when rice is selling at double its ordinary rate.

History of the Famine.—The following paragraphs, showing the effect of the famine of 1866 in Bánkurá, is condensed from the Report of the Famine Commissioners. The price of rice had been high throughout the year 1865 as compared with previous years. In January coarse rice was selling at 25 seers for the rupee, instead of the ordinary rate of 31 or 32 seers. In August 1865 the price was 22 seers against 32 of previous years; and in September, when the failure of the coming crop had become a certainty, a sudden rise to 15 seers took place. In January 1866 the same prices ruled. In February a violent outbreak of cholera occurred, which was assigned to the filthy state of the town and to want of food. The scarcity was attributed to increased exports, and to the dealers withholding their stocks from market. In reply to an application made by the Judge of the District to the Government of Bengal, Rs. 5000 were at once granted from the balance of the North-West Provinces Relief Fund. The Committee resolved to devote these funds entirely to the importation of rice from Calcutta for sale at cost price, with the object of keeping down the artificial prices then ruling, and to bring out the stores which were supposed to exist in this District.

These sales were continued from June to November, at the following rates:—June, $7\frac{1}{2}$ seers per rupee; July, $6\frac{1}{2}$ seers per rupee; August, 6 seers per rupee; September, $5\frac{1}{2}$ seers per rupee; October, $15\frac{1}{4}$ seers per rupee. The fall in price from September to October was extraordinarily sudden. Payments for labour up to July were made in rice, but afterwards in cash. Gratuitous distributions were first made in uncooked, and afterwards in cooked rice. In July the stores in the District failed to supply Bánkurá town, and the Committee reported "no rice in the Bánkurá Bazaar." The Committee then applied for a further grant of Rs. 10,000, for the purchase of rice for retail purposes. On the 23d July the state of things was no better, and the necessity for the grant of Rs. 10,000 was urged on the Commissioner by the Magistrate. A special subscription was raised for the Bishnupur weavers, who were reported "in terrible destitution," for the purpose of supplying them with capital for carrying on their trade and purchasing the produce of their manufactures. A demand of Rs. 5000 was made on their behalf, and Rs. 2000 were granted on this account. In August the Committee applied a third time for a grant of Rs. 10,000, as distress was increasing, and was responded to by the Commissioner, stating that a sum of Rs. 14,000 had been granted for Bánkurá, Bishnupur, and Raniganj, private subscriptions having amounted to Rs. 3000 only. He urged the prosecution of works to give employment, and offered to apply for Rs. 15,000 for this purpose on receipt of detailed proposals for works. The Committee in their reply urged the necessity of a further grant of Rs. 5000, to enable them to carry on where the requirements were increasing. When the new crops came in, the prices fell to 12 seers of rice for the rupee. The aggregate of the weekly total of persons who received gratuitous relief is reported at 47,000, including Raniganj subdivision. The surplus of the Committee's rice realised Rs. 17,425, but was sold below cost price. The total sums placed at the disposal of the Local Relief Committee are returned by the Famine Commissioners as under: Grants by the Board of Revenue, Rs. 12,000; furnished by the Calcutta Relief Committee, Rs. 10,000; Local subscriptions, Rs. 8446; total, Rs. 30,446.

FAMINE WARNINGS.—Scarcity of rain from the beginning of July to the end of August is a warning of famine. The Collector estimates famine rates at double ordinary prices. This would be Rs. 2-8 a maund for rice. Elsewhere he gives Rs. 3 as a famine warning in January; but the price in January 1866 was Rs. 2-10 a maund. The District chiefly depends on the winter or *aman* harvest. *Aus* rice is largely cultivated, but while the *aman* would compensate for the loss of the *aus*, and enable the people to live through the year without famine, the *aus* harvest could never make up for the total loss of the *aman* crop.

MEANS OF TRANSIT.—The means at present at the disposal of the District, if taken in good time, are, in the opinion of the Collector, sufficient to avert the worst consequences of any future famine, by importation from other parts. The railway would afford facilities for the importation of food supplies; but would not guard against danger of isolation of parts of the District situated away from the line of the Trunk road. These outlying tracts are ill provided with means of communication and want both roads and bridges.

The Collector suggests as measures to be adopted for mitigating the evils of famine, the construction of irrigation works by Government, and grants in aid to the landed proprietors for a similar purpose, together with the promotion of emigration.

CULTIVATED AREA.—The total area of the District is returned by the Collector at 864,000 acres, of which 358,046 (*sic*) are under cultivation; 199,904 are capable of cultivation; 11,714 are allowed to lie fallow for one year; and the remainder are waste and uncultivable. The total area under rice cultivation is returned at 467,552 (*sic*) acres; while that under cold-weather crops of pulses or oilseeds is returned at 70,499 acres.

OUT-TURN OF CROPS.—Rice-land paying rent at Rs. 3 is seldom met with in Bánkurá. A fair yield from land paying rent at Rs. 2-6 a *bigha* is returned at 10 maunds of paddy; and for rice-land paying rent at Rs. 1-8 per *bigha*, about 5 maunds of paddy; the price of the paddy being returned at one rupee per maund. Rice-land seldom yields a second crop.

AGRICULTURAL POPULATION.—The Collector of the District furnishes no particulars regarding the proportion of agriculturists to labourers, but the Census Report of 1872 (pp. cxviii.) returns the total "Agricultural and Pastoral Castes" of the Bánkurá District at 91,683, including males, females, and children; exclusive of Musalmáns, aborigines, and semi-Hinduised aborigines partly or wholly living by agriculture. By analysing the details of population arranged according to occupation at pp. cxliv.–cxlvi., I find that the total male adults of class iv., *i.e.*, persons engaged in agriculture or in tending animals, is 77,440. Allowing two other persons as an average of women and children connected with each male adult, the total population living by agriculture or by tending animals amounts to 232,320. Deducting 1489 male adults for the "excepted classes" explained at a foregoing page, *i.e.*, persons possessing lands or otherwise well off, a balance remains of 75,951 males under class iv.; or allowing two other persons to each male adult, a total population of 227,853 souls living by actual husbandry or employed in connection with animals, or tenure-holders belonging to classes who are often people in a small way. This may be taken as the *gross* agricultural population. The total number of male adult "cultivators" as returned by the Census is 69,935, or taking the average of two persons to each male adult as family and children, a *net* cultivating population of 209,805.

The male adults employed in cultivation form more than a fourth of the total males in the District, and the total number of males, females, and children living by cultivation (as estimated by allowing two other persons to each male adult), amounts to 209,805, or about two-fifths of the total population of the District (526,772).

Labouring Population.—The Census Report in its Statement of Castes and Nationalities (pp. cxiv.–cxxii.) returns the labouring classes, below the rank of artisans, of the Bánkurá District, as follows:—

1. Aborigines	44,889
2. Semi-Hinduised aborigines	121,743
3. Personal servant castes	10,019
4. Weaver castes	17,280
5. Labouring castes	11,160
6. Boating and fishing castes	9,618
7. Musicians and vagabond castes	158
8. Unclassified, Vaishnavs, &c.	13,166
Total ...	228,033

Turning to the Statement of Occupations (pp. cxli.–clvii.), I find the following numbers under their respective classes. I only take those who may fairly be considered in the rank of labouring men:—

Class	Occupation	Male Adults.
Class II. (*Professionals*)	Musicians	696
Class III. *Service.*	Personal servants ...	1,408
	Sweepers	14
	Unspecified ...	2,011
Class V. *Conveyance of goods.*	Bullock-drivers ...	35
	Palki-bearers ...	1,022
	Boatmen	1,199

Class VI. *Poorer craftsmen.*	Brick-makers	...	8
	Well-digger	...	1
	Basket-makers	...	377
	Cotton-spinners	...	5
	Weavers in cotton	...	6,685
	Shoe-makers	...	546
Class VII. *Miscellaneous.*	Beggars ...	...	2,444
	Labourers ...	...	41,215
	Unemployed	...	1,576
	Total	...	59,242

The total population of the District is 526,772. Taken by castes, therefore, there are 228,033 persons belonging to the labouring classes, or more than two-fifths of the total population. According to occupation, there are 59,242 male adults, or allowing two other persons to each, a total of 177,726 males, females, and children, being about one-third of the total population. The discrepancy between the results obtained from the Caste and Occupation Statements probably arises from the fact that a large proportion of the aboriginal tribes and semi-Hinduised aboriginals (who are here entered as labourers) are in reality cultivators. But they form the lowest class of husbandmen, and on the approach of famine abandon their fields to seek hired labour, and are thus thrown on the labouring population.

The foregoing calculations yield the following results:—

1.	Total population	526,772
2.	Agriculturists (Hindu) according to caste statement	91,683
3.	Agriculturists (total) according to occupation statement	227,853
4.	Labourers (Hindus) according to caste statement	228,033
5.	Labourers (total) according to occupation statement	177,726
6.	Total agriculturists and labourers (Hindus and aborigines) according to caste statement	319,716
7.	Total agriculturists and labourers (all) according to occupation	405,579

N.B.—It must be remembered that the total of agriculturists and labourers, according to occupation, is obtained by multiplying the number of *male adults* by three.

HUGLI DISTRICT, INCLUDING HOWRAH.

FAMINE PRICES.—The prices current for ordinary rice in 1866 at the principal marts are thus returned by the Famine Commissioners: (1.) Howrah—January, 12 seers for the rupee; February, $10\frac{3}{4}$ seers; March, $10\frac{3}{4}$ seers; April, $10\frac{1}{2}$ seers; May, 10 seers; June, 10 seers; July, $7\frac{15}{16}$ seers; August, $7\frac{3}{4}$ seers; September, $8\frac{1}{8}$ seers; October, $8\frac{9}{16}$ seers; November, $10\frac{11}{16}$ seers; and December, 17 seers for the rupee. (2.) Chandarnagar—January, $14\frac{3}{16}$ seers for the rupee; February, $12\frac{3}{4}$ seers; March, $13\frac{1}{16}$ seers; April, $13\frac{1}{16}$ seers; May, $13\frac{7}{16}$ seers; June, $10\frac{3}{8}$ seers; July, $9\frac{1}{4}$ seers; August, 9 seers; September, $8\frac{3}{16}$ seers; October, $8\frac{7}{8}$ seers; November, $7\frac{9}{16}$ seers; and December, $9\frac{11}{16}$ seers per rupee. (3.) Serampur—January, 12 seers; February, 12 seers; March, $12\frac{1}{4}$ seers; April, $12\frac{1}{4}$ seers; May, $9\frac{1}{2}$ seers; June, $9\frac{1}{4}$ seers; July, 9 seers; August, $8\frac{3}{4}$ seers; September, $8\frac{3}{4}$ seers; October, $8\frac{3}{4}$ seers; November, $14\frac{1}{2}$ seers; and December, $17\frac{3}{4}$ seers. The Magistrate of Howrah gives the following prices as current in 1870:—Best rice, Rs. 3; best paddy Rs. 1-8; ordinary rice, Rs. 2; ordinary paddy, Re. 1 a maund. The Collector of Huglí quotes the rates in 1870 as follows:—Best rice, Rs. 2 to 2-8 per maund; common rice, Rs. 1-12 to Rs. 2-2 per maund; best paddy, Re. 1 to 1-4 per maund; common paddy, from 12 annas to Re. 1 a maund. Prices had then returned to the figure at which they stood previous to the famine. The Collector is of opinion that prices reach famine point when rice sells at Rs. 4 per maund.

FAMINE WARNINGS.—The Collector would consider the failure of three-fourths of the *aman* or winter rice crop as a "sure precursor" of famine.

The District chiefly depends on the *aman* harvest, and the *aus* or autumn crop alone would not enable the people to live throughout the year without actual famine.

MEANS OF TRANSIT.—The roads, railway, canal, and rivers afford means of access to all parts of the District for importation in a famine, which, the Collector reports, could only be caused in this District by a complete drought, or an unexpected general flood at harvest-time. The Ulubáriá irrigation and navigation canal has in some measure remedied the evils of drought, and another canal at right angles to it would, it is considered, render famine practically impossible.

REMEDIAL OR MITIGATING MEASURES.—The evil effects of a drought or unexpected flood could be best capable of remedy or mitigation by the immediate importation of rice into the distressed parts; selling it to those who could buy, and feeding the others gratuitously until the ensuing sowing season, and at the same time supplying seed grain.

Famine in Bengal Proper, the Collector considers, would become impossible, if wheat or any other cold-weather grain, or flesh of animals, were used by the people as food.

CULTIVATED AREA; OUT-TURN OF CROPS.—In the absence of survey papers, the Collector reports that he is unable to give the area of the District, nor do the records contain anything to afford a basis for a reasonable estimate of the comparative acreage of the principal crops. Land paying rent at Rs. 1-8 generally yields from 5 to 7 maunds of paddy per standard *bigha*, and about $\frac{3}{4}$th *kahan* of straw. Land paying rent at Rs. 3 yields about 10 to 12 maunds of paddy per *bigha* and a *kahan* of straw. The price of straw and paddy varies according to the state of the market, but paddy generally sells from Re. 1 to Rs. 1-4 per maund, and straw from Rs. 1-8 to Rs. 2-8 per *kahan*. In the higher classes of the paddy-land *khesari* is sown, and on a very small portion a second crop of rice is reared. The quantity of *khesari* obtained from a *bigha* of land is very variable, but 2 to 3 maunds are the average out-turn, worth about Rs. 2 per maund. The Collector reports that an annual return of Rs. 15 a *bigha* from the best sort of land, and Rs. 10 a *bigha* from the worst, would be considered fair.

HISTORY OF THE FAMINE OF 1866.—The following paragraph is condensed from the Famine Commissioners' Report. In 1865 the scantiness of the crop raised prices in the Húglí District, but nothing like famine was anticipated. In the middle of June the Deputy Magistrate reported great distress in Jahánábád subdivision, and strongly urged the Magistrate to apply for external aid. On the strength of these reports the Magistrate and Collector directed the raising of local subscriptions and the commencement of work, in which proceedings the Commissioner concurred. On the 23d July the Collector applied for a Government grant, but was unsupported by the Commissioner. In August it was found that distress throughout the west of the District was increasing, and in consequence seven centres of relief were organised in the Jahánábád subdivision before the end of August, and cooked food distributed. At this period the two principal classes of sufferers were the labourers who subsisted on wages, and the weavers whose trade had decayed. Of the latter it is estimated that about 6000 emigrated to Calcutta. These, however, were encouraged and assisted to return to their homes, but in course of transit many disappeared. On the 20th of August Mr Turnbull reported from Ghátál that the weavers who had not been to Calcutta refused to do roadwork, and insisted on starting for the city, although informed that their brethren were being sent back. All attempts to make the weavers do roadwork having failed, weaving workshops were set up, in which the men earned from 2 to 4 annas a day, and women only two pice each, a rate insufficient to procure even one meal a day. An attempt was made to insist on labour where possible, but proved a failure. Up to the middle of September the District had received Rs. 17,000 from Calcutta, and on the 6th October the Collector applied for a further grant of Rs. 1500 or 2000, and states that all his demands were promptly complied with. The total amount granted to the Húglí District, including Howrah, for relief, is returned as follows:—

From balance of N. W. P. Fund	Rs.	7,500
From the Calcutta Committee	"	33,900
	"	41,4000
Private subscriptions	"	18,160
Total ...	"	59,560

Agricultural Population.—The Collector does not furnish any particulars regarding the proportion of agriculturists to labourers. But the Census Report of 1872 (p. cxviii.) returns the total "Agricultural and Pastoral Castes" of the District of Húglí with Howrah at 443,561, including males, females, and children; exclusive of Musalmáns and semi-Hinduised aborigines, wholly or partly living by agriculture. By analysing the details of population arranged according to occupation (pp. cxlv., cxlvi.), I find that the total male adults of class iv., *i.e.*, persons engaged in agriculture or in tending animals, is 192,967. Allowing two other persons as an average for women and children connected with each male adult, the total population living by agriculture or by tending animals amounts to 578,901. Deducting 4414 male adults for the "excepted classes" explained at a foregoing page, *i.e.*, persons possessing estates or otherwise well off, a balance remains of 188,553 males under class iv., or allowing two other persons to each male adult, a total population of 565,659 souls living by actual husbandry, or employed in connection with animals, or tenure-holders belonging to classes who are often people in a small way. This may be taken as the *gross* agricultural population. The total number of male adult "cultivators" as returned by the Census is 180,537, or taking the average of two persons to each male adult as women and children, a *net* cultivating population of 541,611.

The male adults employed in cultivation comprise about one-fourth of the total males in the District and the total number of males, females, and children living by cultivation (as estimated by allowing two other persons to each male adult) amounts to 541,611, or over one-third of the total population (1,488,556).

Labouring Population.—The Census Report in its Statement of Castes and Nationalities returns the labouring classes, below the rank of artisans, of the District of Húglí with Howrah, as follows:—

1. Aborigines	968
2. Semi-Hinduised aborigines	260,278
3. Personal servant castes	65,653
4. Weaver castes	53,321
5. Labouring castes	1,390
6. Boating and fishing castes	57,887
7. Musician and vagabond castes	1,636
8. Unclassified, Vaishnavs, &c.	30,148
Total ...	471,281

Turning to the Statement of Occupation (pp. cxli.–clvii.), I find the following numbers under their respective classes:—

Class	Occupation		Male Adults.
Class I. (*Government employ*)	Píyádás ...	...	49
Class II. (*Professionals*)	Musicians ...	...	1,355
Class III. *Service.*	Personal servants	...	6,663
	Sweepers ...	...	300
	Water-carriers	...	144
	Unspecified ...	...	14,269
Class V. *Conveyance of goods.*	Cartmen ...	...	1,583
	Bullock-drivers	...	837
	Palki-bearers ...	...	4,241
	Boatmen ...	...	6,409
Class VI. *Poorer sorts of crafts-men.*	Cane-workers	...	114
	Brick-makers ...	...	687
	Well-diggers ...	...	2
	Basket-makers	...	1,478
	Cotton-carders	...	33
	Weavers in cotton	...	17,049
	Shoe-makers	...	735
	Bird-catchers	...	7
Class VII. *Miscellaneous.*	Beggars and paupers	...	5,750
	Labourers ...	...	79,432
	Unemployed ...	...	18,646
	Total	...	159,783

The total population of the District is 1,488,556. Taken by castes, therefore, there are 471,281 persons belonging to the labouring classes, or about one-third of the total population. According to occupation, there are 159,783 male adults, or allowing two other persons to each, 479,349 males, females, and children, being about one-third of the total population.

The foregoing calculations yield the following *net* results :—

1. Total population	1,488,556
2. Agriculturists (Hindus) according to caste statement	443,561
3. Agriculturists (total) according to occupation	565,659
4. Labourers (Hindus and aborigines) according to caste statement	471,281
5. Labourers (total) according to occupation	479,349

6. Total agriculturists and labourers Hindus and aborigines) according to caste statement 914,842
7. Total agriculturists and labourers (all) according to occupation 1,045,008

N.B.—It must be remembered that the total of agriculturists and labourers, according to occupation, is obtained by multiplying the *male adults* by three.

MIDNAPUR DISTRICT.

FAMINE PRICES.—According to the Famine Commissioners' Report, the following were the average monthly prices of ordinary rice at the principal District marts in 1866:—(1.) Midnapur town—January, 12 seers per rupee; February, 11 seers; March, 11½ seers; April, 10½ seers; May, 9½ seers; June, 9 seers; July, 8 seers; August, 6½ seers; September, 7½ seers; October, 13 seers; November, 24 seers; and December, 22 seers per rupee. (2.) Kespur Mart—January, 15 seers; February, 15 seers; March, 15 seers; April, 12½ seers; May, 10 seers; June, 8¾ seers; July, 6 seers; August, 5 seers; September, 5 seers; October, 10 seers; November, 19 seers; and December, 20 seers per rupee. (3.) Náráyangarh Mart—January, 16 seers per rupee; February, 16 seers; March, 14 seers; April, 14 seers; May, 12 seers; June, 12 seers; July, 8 seers; August, 6 seers; September, 6 seers; October, 10 seers; November, 20 seers; December, 30 seers. The Collector, in his report dated June 1870, states that Government aid becomes necessary when prices rise to Rs. 4 per maund from Rs. 1-8, the ordinary price of rice in Midnapur District. When the price of rice rises to treble the ordinary rates, the Collector considers relief operations become necessary.

HISTORY OF THE FAMINE, condensed from the Famine Commissioners' Report.—The main rice crop of 1865 is estimated at having only yielded half the ordinary out-turn, and in the Jungle Mahals about three-eighths. During September 1865, distress manifested itself in the eastern and southern portions of the District in grain robberies. On the 25th of September the

Deputy Magistrate of Hijili reported that the high prices prevailing in Calcutta were draining away large quantities of rice, and expressed his fears that this circumstance alone might produce famine. On the 4th November the Commissioner recommended that relief works should be put in hand, and that all who were capable of giving labour in return for food should be required to work.

In December, however, the great rice crop of the District was gathered in, and gave a temporary relief from high prices.

In the months of January and February, crime, especially dacoity, increased to an extraordinary degree. In March an asylum was opened in Midnapur for the purpose of providing shelter, clothes, and food for the indigent, and 60 persons were admitted whose condition is described as having been extremely miserable. In April matters became worse, and people were noticed eating water plants and roots not usually considered fit for food, the price of rice in Midnapur itself having risen to 9 seers per rupee. In May the Collector visited the Jungle Mahals, and found that a few deaths from starvation had actually occurred. On the 19th May the Collector returned to Midnapur, and on the 21st submitted to the Board the weekly price current, on which he made the following statement:—"There is no doubt now that deaths from starvation among the old, the weak, and the children are occurring." On receipt of this report the Board granted Rs. 5000 for relief operations in Midnapur. On the 24th May general relief commenced, and upwards of 200 persons applied for relief, "who bore on their bodies the signs of starvation." On the 10th June the Collector received intimation that Government, in the Public Works Department, had assigned Rs. 30,000 for the purpose of being expended on works calculated to afford relief. The average amount earned by men and women was 2 annas each per diem, giving nearly 1 seer of rice per head. The workpeople were never paid in any other form than in money, but at each place where work was in progress the Collector had a depot of rice from which the labourers were supplied. On the 9th July the Collector reported that tolerably good rice was selling at 8 seers per rupee, and that travellers and roadside residents appeared to be as well conditioned as in the most favourable years. Neither the villagers nor the police were aware of any deaths having occurred, and the Collector added that during a four hours' drive only four cases of actual hunger came under his notice, and none of them what might be termed extreme. The Collector estimates that from 10 to 15 per cent. of the population died from starvation or diseases induced by it. The worst suffering was in the portion of the District adjoining Mánbhúm. "There the stonemasons and iron-smelters one and all died. I don't think any relief reached them. They kept to the hills and jungles, and never came near us. Some relief was sent out to a place called Bal-Bahani for them, but it was too late, and when it was sent was insufficient in quantity."

According to figures furnished by the Collector, Rs. 77,350 were received from the Board and the Calcutta Relief Committee, to which Rs. 23,735 were added by subscription. Besides this, 14,300 maunds of rice were supplied to the District at a cost of Rs. 53,034, part of which must have been recovered from sales. The following statement shows the average number of persons relieved daily from June to December 1866:—June, 5155; July, 7442; August, 9606; September, 8752; October, 6476; November, 4247. The sums placed at the disposal of the Relief Committee from May to December were as follow:—Supplied by the Board, Rs. 63,823; Calcutta Relief Committee, 14,000; other subscriptions, 22,874. Total, Rs. 100,697.

FAMINE WARNINGS.—Failure of the local crops, especially of the winter paddy, unusual rise of prices, and absence of importation of paddy from other parts of the country would, in the Collector's opinion, serve as a warning of famine. The lowest rate reported in January 1866 was Rs. 2-8 a maund (see page 146). This may be taken as a warning of famine later in the year.

The District, the Collector states, depends chiefly on the *aman* harvest. The *aus* crop is but an insignificant one in comparison with *aman*. If, therefore, there happened to be a failure of *aman*, *aus* could not make up the loss, and the consequence would be a scarcity amounting to a famine.

MEANS OF TRANSIT.—There are no railways or navigable rivers in the interior of the District. Since the Collector's Report, the Midnapur high-level canal for navigation and irrigation has been opened out. The Collector in 1870 stated that the roads were in tolerably good order, and he considered that to a certain extent they might avert the distress and isolation caused by famine. On this head the only suggestion the Collector could offer was the extension of canals, which he considered should run throughout the District, and have a connection with the navigable rivers of the surrounding Districts.

OUT-TURN OF CROPS.—A fair out-turn from lands paying rent at Rs. 1-8 per *bigha* is returned at 12 maunds of paddy, value Rs. 8, with a second crop, value Rs. 2-8 for land paying Rs. 3 per *bigha*, a fair out-turn is 32 maunds of paddy, value Rs. 21.

CULTIVATED AREA.—The total area of the District is 4836 square miles, or 3,095,040 acres, of which the approximate area under the principal crops is returned as follows:—Pulses and oil seeds, 43,437 acres; and rice, 2,709,923 acres.

AGRICULTURAL POPULATION.—The Collector of the District in his Report gives no information as to the proportion of agriculturists to labourers. But the Census Report of 1872 (pp. cxviii., cxix.) returns the total "Agricultural and Pastoral Castes" (Hindus) of the Midnapur District at 1,063,085, including males, females, and children; but exclusive of the Musalmáns who follow agriculture, and aboriginal or semi-aboriginal tribes, partly living by cultivation. By analysing the details of population arranged according to occupation (pp. cxliv.-cxlvi.), I find that the total male adults of class iv., *i.e.*, persons engaged in agriculture or in tending animals, is 471,949. Allowing two other persons as an average for women and children connected with each male adult, the total population living by agriculture or in connection with animals amounts to 1,415,847. Deducting 6731 male adults for the "excepted classes" explained at a foregoing page, *i.e.*, persons possessing estates, or otherwise well-off, a balance remains of 465,218 males under class iv.; or allowing two other persons to each male adult, a total population of 1,395,654 souls living by husbandry, or employed in connection with animals, or tenure-holders belonging to classes who are often men in a small way. This may be taken as the *gross* agricultural population. The total number of male adult "cultivators" as returned by the Census is 458,515, or taking the average of two persons to each male adult for women and children, a *net* cultivating population of 1,375,545.

The male adults employed in cultivation form about three-eighths of the total number of males in the District; and the total number of males, females, and children living by cultivation, as estimated by allowing two other persons to each male adult, amounts to 1,375,545, or more than half the total population of the District (2,540,963).

LABOURING POPULATION.—The Census Report in its statement of Castes and Nationalities (pp. cxiv.–cxxiii.), returns the labouring classes, below the rank of artisans of the Midnapur District as follows. The figures have been corrected from the subsequent District Census Statements by Mr C. F. Magrath :—

1. Aborigines	139,108
2. Semi-Hinduised aboriginals	244,705
3. Personal servant castes	90,195
4. Weaver castes	141,770
5. Labouring castes	24,833
6. Boating and fishing castes	90,374
7. Beggar and vagabond castes	2,444
8. Unspecified, Vaishnavs, &c.	122,471
Total ...	855,900

Turning to the Statement of Occupations (pp. cxli.–clvii.), I find the following numbers under their respective classes. I only take those who may fairly be considered in the rank of labouring men :—

Class	Occupation	MALE ADULTS.
Class I. (*Government Employ*)	Píyádás ...	129
Class II. (*Professionals*)	Musicians	2,032
Class III. *Service.*	Personal servants ...	15,960
	Sweepers ...	235
	Water-carriers ...	63
	Unspecified ...	378
Class V. *Conveyance of goods.*	Cartmen ...	164
	Bullock-drivers ...	242
	Palki-bearers ...	5,182
	Boatmen... ...	6,509
Class VI. *Poorer sorts of craftsmen.*	Cane-workers ...	41
	Brick-makers ...	79
	Basket-makers ...	2,122
	Cotton-weavers ...	26,276
	Shoe-makers ...	886

Class VII. *Miscellaneous.*		
	Beggars ...	18,998
	Labourers ...	115,308
	Unemployed ...	15,830
	Total ...	210,434

The total population of the District is 2,540,963. Taken by castes, therefore, there are 855,900 persons belonging to the labouring classes, or about one-third of the total population. According to occupation, there are 210,434 male adults, or 631,302 males, females, and children, being about one-fourth of the total population.

The discrepancy between the figures obtained for the labourers from the Caste and Occupation Statements, probably arises from the fact that a large proportion of the aboriginal and semi-aboriginal tribes (who are here entered as labourers) are in reality cultivators. But they form the lowest class of husbandmen, and on the approach of famine abandon their fields to seek hired labour, and are thus thrown on the labouring population.

The foregoing calculations yield the following results:—

1. Total population	2,540,963
2. Agriculturists (Hindus) according to castes	1,063,085
3. Agriculturists according to occupation (all)	1,395,654
4. Labouring population according to caste (Hindus, aborigines, and semi-aborigines)	855,900
5. Labouring population according to occupation (all)	631,302
6. Total agriculturists and labourers, according to caste statement (Hindus, &c.) ...	1,918,985
7. Total agriculturists and labourers according to occupation statement (all)	2,026,956

N.B.—It must be remembered that the total of agriculturists and labourers, according to occupation, is obtained bymultiplying the number of male adults by three.

CHOTA NAGPUR DIVISION.

HAZARIBAGH DISTRICT.

Famine Prices.—The Deputy Commissioner, in his report dated 9th February 1871, returns the maximum prices of rice and paddy during the famine of 1866 as follows:—Best cleaned rice, Rs. 7 per maund; common rice, Rs. 5; best paddy, Rs. 3-8; and common paddy, Rs. 2-8 per maund. Local prices had not returned in 1871 to their ordinary rates previous to the famine; nor does the Deputy Commissioner think they will ever quite come down to those rates.

Famine Warnings.—The Deputy Commissioner considers that prices fail to yield any warning of famine, as the people of the District have three crops, and not merely one. In the cold weather, besides wheat and barley, *gram*, *kulthi*, and *arhar* are grown; in spring (May and June) Indian corn, *janirah*, *mahua*, and millets. In autumn there is the rice crop. A deficiency in the rice harvests for two years, followed by no rain in the cold weather, should be considered a warning of distress, and possibly of famine. A further cause for apprehension would be the failure of the early rain, causing the failure of the Indian corn, *janirah*, and *mahua* crops. Many of the common descriptions of grain never come into the market, consequently the Deputy Commissioner thinks that merely recording the prices would afford no adequate criterion. In 1866, when the greatest scarcity in the memory of man occurred in the District, the price of rice did not rise above 10 seers per rupee previous to the commencement of relief operations. Even then the distress was only among the poorest classes, such as the day labourers, who had been turned adrift by their employers. The agricultural classes, as a body, though obliged to be very careful, and even to stint themselves somewhat in food, were never in danger of starvation. The Deputy Commissioner reports to me that one crop saved out of the three would enable the people to live through the year without absolute famine.

MEANS OF TRANSIT.—The great want of the District is roads. The absence of such means of communication would, in the opinion of the Deputy Commissioner, prove very serious for certain portions of the District, which would be liable to isolation in time of famine. Importation of food would be impossible except in the cold weather. Absolute famine, however, although possible, is considered scarcely probable.

CULTIVATED AREA.—The total area of the District is returned by the Deputy Commissioner at 4,493,319 acres, made up as follows:—Under cultivation, 1,334,876 acres; uncultivated, but capable of cultivation, 2,790,425 acres; under jungle and uncultivable, 368,018 acres.

Of the cultivated area, 624,128 acres are under rice. Barley and wheat take up 20,388 acres; and Indian corn, 531,538 acres. There are a few exceptional cases of land paying rent at Rs. 3 per *bigha*, but generally Rs. 2-8 per *bigha* is the rate for the best paddy land.

AGRICULTURAL POPULATION.—The Deputy Commissioner in his report gives no particulars regarding the proportion of agriculturists to labourers. But the Census Report of 1872 (p. cxxxvi.) returns the total "Agricultural and Pastoral Castes" (Hindus) of the Hazáríbágh District at 175,222, including males, females, and children; but exclusive of Musalmàns, aborigines, and semi-Hinduised aboriginal tribes wholly or partly living by agriculture. By analysing the details of population arranged according to occupation (pp. clxix., clxx.), I find that the total male adults of class iv., *i.e.*, persons engaged in agriculture or in tending animals, is 143,452. Allowing two other persons as an average of women and children connected with each male adult, the total population living by agriculture or by tending animals amounts to 430,356. Deducting 4617 male adults for the "excepted classes" explained at a foregoing page, *i.e.*, persons possessing estates, or otherwise well off, a balance remains of 138,835 males under class iv.; or allowing two other persons to each male adult, a total population of 416,505 souls living by actual husbandry, or employed in connection with animals, or tenure-holders belonging to classes who are often people in a small way. This may be taken as the *gross* agricultural population. The total number of male adult "cultivators" as returned by the Census is 137,142, or taking the average of two persons to each male adult as women and children, a *net* cultivating population of 411,426.

The male adults employed in cultivation comprise over one-third of the total males in the District; and the total number of males, females, and children living by cultivation (as estimated by allowing two other persons to each male adult) amounts to 411,426, or about four-sevenths of the total population of the District (771,875).

LABOURING POPULATION.—The Census Report in its Statement of Castes and Nationalities (pp. cxxxiv.–cxxxvii.) returns the labouring classes, below the rank of artisans, of the Hazáríbágh District as follow. The figures have been verified from the subsequent District Census Statements compiled by Mr C. F. Magrath :—

1. Aborigines	57,120
2. Semi-Hinduised aborigines	216,712
3. Personal servant castes	49,055
4. Weaver castes	2,608
5. Labouring castes	2,793
6. Boating and fishing castes	2,209
7. Musician and vagabond castes	112
8. Unclassified, Vaishnavs, &c.	3,473
Total ...	334,082

Turning to the Statement of Occupations (pp. clxv.–clxxix.), I find the following numbers under their respective classes. I only take those who may fairly be considered in the rank of labouring men :—

		MALE ADULTS.
Class I. (*Government employ*)	Píyádás	34
Class II. (*Professionals*)	Musicians	98
Class III. *Service.*	Personal servants ...	3,038
	Sweepers	83
	Water-carriers ...	20
Class V. *Conveyance of persons or goods.*	Cartmen	31
	Bullock-drivers ...	243
	Palki-bearers ...	253

Class VI. *Poorer craftsmen.*	Basket-makers	...	676
	Cotton-spinners	...	1,636
	Cotton-carders	...	25
	Bird-catchers	...	4
Class VII. *Miscellaneous.*	Beggars ...	...	1,663
	Labourers ...	...	54,173
	Unemployed	...	1,948
	Total	...	63,925

The total population of the District is 771,875. Taken by castes, therefore, there are 334,082 persons belonging to the labouring classes, or three-sevenths of the total population. According to occupation, there are 63,925 male adults, or allowing two other persons to each, 191,775 males, females, and children, being about one-fourth of the total population. The discrepancy between the results obtained from the Caste and Occupation Statements probably arises from the fact that a large proportion of aboriginal and semi-aboriginal tribes (who are here entered as labourers) are in reality cultivators. But they form the lowest class of husbandmen; and, on the approach of famine, abandon their fields to seek hired labour, and are thus thrown on the labouring population.

The foregoing calculations yield the following results:—

1. Total population	771,875
2. Agriculturists (Hindus) according to caste statement	175,222
3. Agriculturists (total) according to occupation statement	416,505
4. Labourers (Hindus and aborigines) according to caste statement	334,082
5. Labourers (total) according to occupation	191,775
6. Total agriculturists (Hindus and aborigines) according to caste statement	509,304
7. Total agriculturists and labourers (all) according to occupation	608,280

N.B.—It must be remembered that the total of agriculturists and labourers, according to occupation, is obtained by multiplying the *male adults* by three.

LOHARDAGA DISTRICT.

FAMINE PRICES.—The prices of rice and paddy during the famine of 1866 are returned to me by the Deputy Commissioner as follows:—Best cleaned rice from Rs. 4-1 to Rs. 4-2 per maund; common rice from Rs. 3-8 to Rs. 3-12 per maund; best paddy from Rs. 2 to Rs. 2-10 per maund; common paddy from Rs. 1-12 to Rs. 1-14. Prices for other food grains prevailing in 1866 are thus returned:—Unshelled barley, from Rs. 4-13 to Rs. 5 per maund; Indian corn, Rs. 2-2 to Rs. 2-8 per maund; and wheat, Rs. 4-13 to Rs. 5 per maund. The Deputy Commissioner, in his report, dated February 1871, stated that local prices had not then returned to their ordinary rates previous to the famine. He considered, however, that they were returning to their original standard, and had no doubt of their doing so, provided one or two average seasons ensued. The ordinary prices of food grains in 1870 is returned as under:—Best cleaned rice, Rs. 2 to Rs. 2-2 per maund; common rice, Rs. 1-4 to Rs. 1-8 per maund; barley, Rs. 1-6 to Rs. 1-9 per maund; Indian corn, 12 to 14 annas per maund; wheat, Rs. 2 to Rs. 2-8 per maund.

FAMINE WARNINGS.—Lohárdágá District consists of two distinct tracts of country, having different features, and growing different crops—namely, that known as Chotá Nágpur proper, and the subdivision of Palámau. I extract the following regarding famine prices and famine warnings in the District, from a report furnished to me in 1871 by the Deputy Commissioner:—

"First as regards Chotá Nágpur.—This is a great rice-growing country, and rice is the staple grain, both among the Aryan and non-Aryan population. The rice crop, as elsewhere, is composed both of highland and lowland crops, but the country undoubtedly depends chiefly on the latter, the highland, or *aus* crop could by no possibility ever make up for a total loss of the lowland or *aman* crop. The produce of the former crop, I should roughly estimate, is always somewhat less than one-fourth of the lowland or *aman* rice. It is brought for sale at the local markets during the month of September and October, after which it is hardly procurable. Whatever balance remains is stored up in small quantities by the cultivators for seed. With regard to the precise point at which scarcity may be said to amount to famine, or the point at which Government relief operations become necessary,—this is a question which appears to me to depend upon such a variety of circumstances that it seems almost impossible to say where scarcity ends, and where famine begins, more particularly so in a vast wild country like this, where it is so difficult to obtain anything approaching to reliable local information. In the year 1866, while famine was raging in the District of Mánbhúm on the east, and the District of Gayá on the north-west, there was no famine prevalent here. Prices rose very considerably, however, and no doubt in some parts people were much pushed; but there was no actual famine except in one or two places quite on the borders of Mánbhúm. The high prices were caused in consequence of the enormous quantity of grain which was being exported from the District to Behar and elsewhere. Had the crops happened to have failed here as they did in Mánbhúm, the famine would no doubt have spread here, and in that case local prices would have risen still higher than they did. In attempting, therefore, to fix the point at which relief operations may become necessary, I am inclined to take the prices then prevalent partly as a guide, and after considering them, together with the price of wages and the character of the people, I am of opinion that when coarse rice cannot be procured for less than Rs. 4-8 per maund, and the corresponding kind of paddy for less than Rs. 2-12 per maund, then the point at which scarcity amounts to famine would be reached, and Government relief would be necessary.

"It is possible, however, that under certain circumstances the people might be able to hold out beyond these prices, and on the other hand it is by no means impossible that under other circumstances scarcity would turn to famine before those prices were reached. For instance, I find that famine was prevalent in the subdivision of Palámau during the year 1859-60, when relief operations were carried on on a considerable scale, although rice and paddy were both selling then at a cheaper rate than in 1866-67, when no actual famine was felt. Coarse rice and coarse paddy were in 1859 and 1860 selling respectively at Rs. 3-5-4 and Rs. 1-10-6 per maund, as compared with Rs. 3-12-2 and Rs. 1-14-1 in 1866-67. This perhaps may be said to tend to show that the point which I have fixed as famine point is too high, inasmuch as on the occasion above adverted to famine existed when the rates were very much lower. My remarks, however, were confined exclusively to Chotá Nágpur, which is a rice-growing country, and were not intended to refer to Palámau, which cannot be called a rice-growing country. These show the great difficulty which exists in arriving at anything like a correct conclusion on such a question, and I am unable to account for the difference in the Palámau rates on the two occasions referred to.

"With regard to what may be considered warnings of famine, I am of opinion that in this part of the country everything may be said to depend on the lowland or *aman* crop. Other crops may fail, but if there be no failure of the lowland crops there can be no famine. On the other hand, I do not think that a good crop of highland or *aus* paddy and Indian corn would be sufficient to keep off famine in the event of a total failure of the lowland crop, though they might no doubt do so in the event of only a partial failure. Thus if the *aus* rice and Indian corn harvest were to fail, and the weather were to appear for some time unpropitious for the lowland crop, there would no doubt be reason to apprehend the probability of distress; also, if immediately upon the latter harvest being reaped, the price of rice suddenly increased to 16 seers per rupee, or Rs. 2-8 per maund, there would be every reason to apprehend that about the month of March or April it would be selling as high as Rs. 5 per maund, in which case relief operations would be necessary.

"With respect to the subdivision of Palámau, I have already remarked that it differs considerably from Chotá Nágpur Proper in its crops. In Palámau a great portion of the inhabitants do not depend on rice as their staple article of food, as they do in Chotá Nágpur. The Assistant Commissioner in charge of the subdivision, who has had several years' experience, remarks in connection with this subject that the population of Palámau is nearly equally divided into two distinct sections of people—the Aryan population, whose staple article of food is rice; and the non-Aryan, who depend chiefly on the crops of the autumn harvest, and to whom Indian corn and the *mahua* fruit may be said to be staple articles of food. Both classes are, of course, affected by famine, but while one may be seriously affected, little or no inconvenience may be felt by the other. For instance, in the event of a total failure of the three harvests, viz., the autumn rice and Indian corn, the winter rice crop, and the spring harvest of pulses, &c., as well as of the *mahua* crop, the position of the aboriginal section of the community would be more critical than that of the Aryan, inasmuch as while the former are almost entirely dependent on those crops, all of which are produced in Palámau, the latter are dependent for the greater portion of the rice they consume on importations from other Districts, the actual produce of rice being very small in proportion to the consumption. Consequently, a total failure of the local rice crop, even if prices were low and the stock ample in the exporting Districts of Behar, would cause inconvenience by a considerable rise in prices, but would not amount to famine height.

"If, on the other hand, the failure of the rice crop be accompanied by a general failure in the surrounding Districts, then doubtless the rice-eating section of the community would suffer from famine; although, as stated before, the aborigines would suffer great privation in the event of the failure of the Indian corn harvest and *mahua* fruit, still so long as rice is cheap and plentiful they could always tide over their difficulties. If, however, a failure of the rainy crops was to be accompanied by a failure, or even a partial failure, of the rice crop, prices would rise beyond their means, and the result, it is feared, would be something very like famine. The aboriginal tribes, however, have this advantage, that they are capable of subsisting on many kinds of jungle fruits and herbs (some, indeed, do it from choice); but there can be no doubt that little short of starvation would drive them to it for their entire subsistence.

"With regard to the warnings of famine, the Assistant Commissioner of Palámau is of opinion that an indifferent Indian corn crop and rice harvest in one year, followed by the failure of the *mahua* crop in March, together with a scarcity of rainfall in June and July, and general high prices prevailing in the surrounding Districts, would give rise to serious apprehensions, and would be sufficient grounds for anticipating so early as August a great scarcity, if not absolute famine. The symptoms of distress would begin to make themselves felt about the middle of January, when the prices of coarse rice, coarse paddy, Indian corn, and *mahua* might be expected to stand respectively at Rs. 3-8, Rs. 1-12, Rs. 2-12, and Rs. 2-8 per standard maund. A good *mahua* crop following in March would afford partial relief, but if this crop again failed, relief operations would in all probability have to be continued until the end of July or middle of August."

MEANS OF TRANSIT.—"With regard to the means available

for averting the extremity of famine by importation, there are no railways, navigable rivers, or canals in this District, but there are roads and plenty of pack-bullocks always going and coming. As long as the famine is only local, and does not extend at the same time to all the surrounding Districts, the means of importation are sufficient. In the case, however, of a general failure of crops both here and in the surrounding Districts, this part of the country would be in considerable danger of isolation, unless grain was actually to be imported by the Government."

CULTIVATED AREA.—The Deputy Commissioner returns the area under cultivation at 2,824,320 acres; 2,174,080 acres as cultivable but not under tillage; and 2,290,560 acres uncultivable and waste. He states that it is impossible to form even an approximate estimate of the comparative acreage under the principal crops. The area under rice equals, if it does not exceed, the acreage under all the other crops put together.

OUT-TURN OF CROPS.—The Deputy Commissioner states that it is difficult to estimate the out-turn of paddy per *bigha* as regards Lohárdágá District. In the part of the District known as Chotá Nágpur Proper, land is generally measured by the quantity of seed sown.

A fair yield from first-quality land is said to be 5 maunds 9 seers of paddy per *bigha*, and that of the second quality 3 maunds 35 seers per *bigha*. Both descriptions of land paid an average rent of 13 annas per *bigha;* the reason assigned for this anomaly being that, in good seasons, both yielded an equal crop. This, however, the Deputy Commissioner can scarcely believe to be the case. As a rule, second crops are not grown. In the case of a few highlands, at the foot of the hills, *musuri*, barley, and gram are occasionally grown in addition to paddy.

AGRICULTURAL POPULATION.—The Deputy Commissioner roughly estimates the proportion of agriculturists to labourers as seven to one. But the Census Report of 1872 (p. cxxxvi.) returns the total "Agricultural and Pastoral Castes" (Hindus) of Lohárdágá District at 144,053, including males, females, and children; but exclusive of the Musalmáns who follow agriculture, and aboriginal or semi-aboriginal tribes partly living by cultivation. But by analysing the details of population arranged according to occupation (pp. clxv.-clxxix.), I find that the total male adults of class iv., *i.e.*, persons engaged in agriculture or with animals, is 236,624. Allowing two other persons as an average for women and children connected with each male adult, the total population living by agriculture or by tending animals amounts to 709,872. Deducting 7953 male adults for the "excepted classes" explained at a foregoing page, *i.e.*, persons possessing estates or otherwise well off, a balance remains of 228,671 males under class iv.; or allowing two other persons to each male adult, a total population of 686,013 souls living by husbandry or employed in connection with animals, or tenure-holders belonging to classes who are often people in a small way. This may be taken as the *gross* agricultural population. The total number of male adult "cultivators" as returned by the Census is 222,798, or taking the average of two persons to each male adult as women and children, a *net* agricultural population of 668,394.

The male adults employed in cultivation form about three-eighths of the total males in the District; and the total number of males, females, and children living by cultivation (as estimated by allowing two other persons to each male adult) amounts to 668,394, or more than half of the total population of the District (1,237,123).

LABOURING POPULATION.—The Census Report in its Statement of Castes and Nationalities (pp. cxxxiv.-cxxxvii.) returns the labouring classes, below the rank of artisans, of the Lohárdágá District, as follow. The figures have been corrected from the subsequent District Census Statements by Mr C. F. Magrath:—

1. Aboriginal tribes	518,645
2. Semi-Hinduised aborigines	225,173
3. Personal servant castes	45,178
4. Weaver castes	9,897
5. Labouring castes	3,581
6. Boating and fishing castes	9,091
7. Musician and vagabond castes	281
8. Unspecified, Vaishnavs, &c.	23,487
Total ...	835,333

Turning to the Statement of Occupation (pp. clxv.-clxxix.), I find the following numbers under their respective classes. I only take those who may fairly be considered in the rank of labouring men:—

Class	Occupation	MALE ADULTS.
Class I. (*Government employ*)	Píyádás	220
Class II. (*Professionals*)	Musicians	1,668
Class III. *Service.*	Personal servants	4,118
	Sweepers	40
	Water-carriers	5
	Unspecified	9,127
Class V. *Conveyance of goods.*	Bullock-drivers	396
	Palki-bearers	73
	Boatmen	75
Class VI. *Poorer sorts of craftsmen.*	Brick-makers	5
	Lime-burners	9
	Digger	1
	Basket-makers	2,098
	Cotton-spinners	11,473
	Cotton-carders	270
Class VII. *Miscellaneous.*	Beggars	2,140
	Labourers	43,713
	Unemployed	228
	Total	75,659

The total population of the District is 1,237,123. Taken by castes, therefore, there are 835,333 persons belonging to the labouring classes, or more than two-thirds of the total population. According to occupation, there are 75,659 male adults who may fairly be considered in the rank of labouring men, or 226,977 males, females, and children, being above one-sixth part of the total population. The discrepancies between the results obtained from the Caste and Occupation Statements probably arise from the fact that a large proportion of the aboriginal and semi-aboriginal tribes (who are entered by caste as labourers) are in reality cultivators. But they form the lowest class of husbandmen, and on the approach of famine abandon their fields to seek hired labour, and are thus thrown on the labouring population.

The foregoing calculations give the following results:—

1. Total population	1,237,123
2. Agriculturists (Hindus) according to caste statement	144,053

3. Total agriculturists according to occupation statement	686,013
4. Labourers (Hindus, aborigines, &c.) according to caste	835,333
5. Labourers (total) according to occupation	226,977
6. Total of agriculturists and labourers (Hindus, aborigines, &c.) according to caste ...	979,386
7. Total of agriculturists and labourers (all) according to occupation	912,990

N.B.—It must be remembered that the total of agriculturists and labourers, according to occupation, is obtained by multiplying the number of male adults by three.

SINGHBHUM DISTRICT.

FAMINE PRICES.—In the Report of the Famine Commissioners the price of rice in 1866 is returned as follows:—January, 14 seers per rupee; February, 12 seers; March, 12 seers; April, 12 seers; May, 9 seers; June, 6 seers; July, 5½ seers; August, 5 seers; September, 7 seers; October, 16 seers; November, 16 seers; December, 16 seers per rupee.

The Deputy Commissioner, in his report to me, dated May 1871, states that the prices had then returned to the ordinary rates prevailing before the famine.

FAMINE WARNINGS.—If the yield of the cold-weather or *aman* harvest were less than half the usual out-turn, and prices reached 12 to 16 seers per rupee in January, it should be a warning of famine later in the year. The roads and means of communication are reported adequate to prevent isolation.

REMEDIAL MEASURES.—The Deputy Commissioner suggests the early organisation of relief works for the labouring classes, and considers that assistance should, as far as possible, come from the more fortunate of the people themselves; he declares indiscriminate help from the State to be mischievous and demoralising.

CULTIVATED AREA.—The total area of the District is returned at 4503 square miles, of which 852,480 acres were returned in 1871 as cultivated; 1,136,740 acres as uncultivated, but capable of being brought under tillage; and 892,700 acres as uncultivable and waste. The Deputy Commissioner estimates the comparative acreage under principal crops as follows:—Rice, 503,233 acres; Indian corn, 63,029 acres; wheat, 1271 acres; pulses, 3813 acres; cotton, 23,637 acres; and oil seeds, 40,665 acres.

OUT-TURN OF CROPS.—A good out-turn from the best lands is returned at 15 maunds of paddy per *bigha*, value Rs. 7-8; inferior land, 12 maunds per *bigha*, value Rs. 4-8. The Deputy Commissioner says that he does not know whether it is possible to grow a second crop, but thinks that only one crop of paddy is obtained from the same land.

AGRICULTURAL POPULATION.—The Deputy Commissioner of the District furnishes no particulars regarding the proportion of agriculturists to labourers. But the Census Report of 1872 (p. cxxxvi.) returns the total "Agricultural and Pastoral Castes" (Hindus) of the Singhbhúm District at 58,288, including males, females, and children; exclusive of Musalmáns and aboriginal and semi-Hinduised aboriginal tribes wholly or partly living by agriculture. By analysing the details of population arranged according to occupation (pp. clxv.–clxxix.), I find that the total male adults of class iv., *i.e.*, persons engaged in agriculture or with animals, is 74,666. Allowing two other persons as an average for women and children connected with each male adult, the total population living by agriculture or by tending animals amounts to 223,998. Deducting 1611 male adults for the "excepted classes" explained at a foregoing page, *i.e.*, persons possessing estates or otherwise well off, a balance remains of 73,005 males under class iv., or allowing two other persons to each male adult, a total population of 219,015 souls living by actual husbandry or employed in connection with animals, or tenure-holders belonging to classes who are often people in a small way. This may be taken as the *gross* agricultural population. The total number of male adult "cultivators" as returned by the Census is 71,393, or taking the average of two persons to each male adult, a total *net* cultivating population of 214,179.

The male adults employed in cultivation form more than one-third of the total males in the District, and the total number of males, females, and children living by cultivation (as estimated by allowing two other persons to each male adult) amounts to 214,179, or above one-half of the total population (415,023).

LABOURING POPULATION.—The Census Report in its Statement of Castes and Nationalities (pp. cxxxiv.–cxxxvii.) returns the labouring classes, below the rank of artisans, of the Singhbhúm District, as follows. The figures have been verified from the District Census Statements :—

1. Aboriginal tribes	256,065
2. Semi-Hinduised aboriginals	28,747
3. Personal servant castes	4,146
4. Weaver castes	21,773
5. Labouring castes	826
6. Boating and fishing castes	2,091
7. Unclassified, Vaishnavs, &c.	3,845
Total ...	317,493

Turning to the Statement of Occupation (pp. clxv.–clxxix.), I find the following numbers :—

Class I. (*Government employ*)	Píyádás ...	6
Class II. (*Professionals*)	Musicians ...	80
Class III. *Service.*	Personal servants	1,097
	Sweepers ...	14
	Water-carriers ...	95
	Unspecified ...	4,407
Class V. *Conveyance of goods.*	Cartman ...	1
	Bullock-driver ...	1
	Boatmen ...	19
Class VI. *Poorer sorts of craftsmen.*	Basket-makers ...	366
	Cotton-spinners	2,772
	Shoe-makers ...	24
Class VII. *Miscellaneous.*	Beggars ...	655
	Labourers ...	28,401
	Unemployed ...	160
	Total ...	38,098

The total population of the District is 415,023. Taken by castes, therefore, there are 317,493 persons belonging to the labouring classes, or about three-fourths of the total population. According to occupation, there are 38,098 male adults, or allowing two other persons to each, 114,294, or two-sevenths of the total population. The discrepancy between the results obtained from the Caste and Occupation Statements probably arises from the fact that a large proportion of the aboriginal tribes (entered by caste as labourers) in reality live by agriculture. They, however, form the lowest class of husbandmen, and although in the event of a famine they can hold out for a short time by hunting, or living upon jungle fruits and roots, these shifts soon become precarious, and they are thrown on the labouring population.

The foregoing calculations give these results:—

1. Total population	415,023
2. Agriculturists (Hindus) according to caste statement	58,288
3. Agriculturists (total) according to occupation	219,015
4. Labourers (Hindus and aborigines) according to caste statement	317,493
5. Labourers (total) according to occupation	114,294
6. Total agriculturists and labourers (Hindus and aborigines) according to caste statement	375,781
7. Total agriculturists and labourers (all) according to occupation	333,309

N.B.—It should always be remembered that the total of agriculturists and labourers according to occupation is obtained by multiplying the male *adults* by three.

MANBHUM DISTRICT.

Famine Prices.—The Report of the Famine Commissioners returns the rates current for rice and paddy in Mánbhúm District during each month of the famine year of 1866 as follows:— January, 13 seers per rupee; February, 13 seers; March, 13 seers; April, 13 seers; May, 10 seers; June, 8½ seers; July, 5 seers; August, 5 seers; September, 5½ to 6 seers; October,

8 seers; November, 16 seers; December, 26 seers per rupee. The highest price of Indian corn was 12 seers per rupee. The current rates, as quoted by the Deputy Commissioner in his report, dated June 1871, were as follow:—Best cleaned rice, Rs. 18 to 20 seers per rupee; common quality, 25 to 30 seers per rupee; paddy, best quality, one rupee per maund; common quality, one and a half maunds per rupee; wheat, 12 seers per rupee; Indian corn, 1¼ maunds per rupee. The Deputy Commissioner reported in 1871 that local prices might be considered as having returned to the rates which ruled before the famine. The average daily number of persons who received relief during the famine, from the months of June to December inclusive, is thus returned by the Famine Commissioners:—June, 322; July, 1262; August, 2831; September, 5825; October, 9630; November, 4253; and December, 1925.

The sums placed at the disposal of the Relief Committee were —from the Board of Revenue, Rs. 43,346; from the Calcutta Relief Committee, Rs. 28,200; other subscriptions, Rs. 4814; total, Rs. 76,360.

FAMINE WARNINGS.—The Deputy Commissioner considers absence of rain after the transplanting and sowing of the crops, with excess of rain during the months of October and November, to be famine warnings. He would also consider famine imminent were paddy to rise to 30 seers and rice to 15 seers per rupee during the months of January or February. The District depends chiefly on the *aman* harvest, and were that to fail, the Deputy Commissioner does not think the *aus* could make up for it.

MEANS OF TRANSIT.—If the roads were completed, there are ample supplies of carts and pack-bullocks in the District for the purposes of importation, which, in the Deputy Commissioner's opinion, would be the only means of importation. The south-western portion of the District is liable to isolation, but this could be averted by the construction of a road in that direction.

REMEDIAL OR MITIGATING MEASURES.—The best and only means of preventing or alleviating famine is, in the opinion of the Deputy Commissioner, the construction of roads, by which food could be rapidly and cheaply distributed to the localities suffering from want of food. Canals would have the same effect, but he reports that roads are more urgently required, as being made more quickly, and at a less expenditure.

Out-turn of Crops.—For land paying Rs. 1-8 per standard *bigha*, a yield of from 8 to 10 maunds of paddy per *bigha* is considered a fair out-turn, and from that paying Rs. 3, from 16 to 20 maunds of paddy. A second crop is rarely raised, and only from the higher-priced land. A fair return for a whole year for a *bigha* of land renting at Rs. 1-8 might be estimated at 8 maunds of produce, value Rs. 5-5-4.

History of the Famine of 1866, condensed from the Famine Commissioners' Report.—The crops of 1863 and 1864 were short ones, and the early rice crop of 1865 was injured by excessive rain. The price of coarse rice had been steadily rising since 1863, and in August 1866 reached a maximum of 5 seers per rupee. The cold-weather crop of 1865 only gave an out-turn of between one-third and half of a full crop, and over a considerable tract the yield could not have exceeded one-fourth. In December 1865 the Deputy Commissioner proposed to form a Relief Fund by using a subscription of Rs. 800. On the 15th March the District Superintendent of Police reported great increase of crime, and the evident distress which was the cause of it. He recommended the expenditure of a few thousand rupees on public works, which would give subsistence to many who were driven to dacoity and robbery. This proposition, however, was rejected by the Deputy Commissioner, who adduced as his reason the fact that considerable sums were already being expended on works in the District without producing any perceptible effect. Paddy was selling on the 7th May at 18 to 20 seers for the rupee.

Towards the end of May 1866 crime increased to such an extent that scarcely a night passed without some house being attacked and grain plundered. On the 28th May the Board of Revenue sent Rs. 2000 to the Dy. Commissioner to be employed through the agency of the Local Committee, with a view to stimulate private liberality. On the 22d May the Committee, having Rs. 3000 at their disposal, resolved to begin works on a scale sufficient to employ 500 men and 500 women daily on them. On 30th May, after the receipt of the grant of Rs. 2000 from the Board, the Committee resolved to open depots for gratuitous relief in the south of the District, and to devote the Government grant to these, while the subscriptions were devoted to the employment of labour. It was resolved that at each centre 150 persons should receive half a seer of rice daily. Up to the 5th June employment had been provided for 1000 persons, and gratuitous relief for 450. This was little in comparison with the requirements, but the funds at disposal were totally inadequate to meet them fully. At the chief market in Barábhúm prices had suddenly risen from 11 to 9 seers for the rupee. The grain-dealers bought up all the rice they could, and then closed their shops until the people paid any price they asked. At this time dacoities were taking place at the rate of four every night. Rice now rose to 7½ seers per rupee. On the 11th the Deputy Commissioner reported to the Committee that the means at their disposal would not effect one-twentieth of what was required. The immediate effect of the opening of the depots in the south was a marked decrease in grain-robberies. Before the end of June the Board had allotted a further grant of Rs. 5000, and had promised to send up 5000 maunds of rice at once. On the 25th June the Assistant Magistrate of the Govindpur subdivision reported a sudden rise in the price of rice from 11 to 7½ seers per rupee, and Rs. 500 were sent to him by the Mánbhúm Committee. At this time the people were living on the seeds of the *sal* tree, chaff of rice, oilcake, &c. In June the Government in the Public Works Department granted Rs. 4000 for the employment of the able-bodied on the roads. In the middle of July the persons receiving relief daily at all depots numbered 1900. Deaths were taking place in the streets of Puruliá, and the Committee determined to open a special hospital. In August distress and mortality were increasing rapidly all over the District, and at the end of the month rice was selling at Puruliá at the rate of 4 and 4½ seers to the rupee. The Deputy Commissioner found himself compelled to sell at 7½ seers from the stores to save the poorer respectable classes, who were succumbing to cholera from eating bad food. In the latter end of the month of October the Deputy Commissioner found that mortality had much decreased since the opening of regular depots on a large scale. About the 29th September an application was made for Rs. 10,000, and money was again asked for in October by the Deputy Commissioner, but not receiving it, he made an advance to the Committee from his private funds. On the 3d November rice was selling at 20 seers per rupee, and distress rapidly decreasing. On the 14th November a sum of Rs. 8000 was received from the Calcutta Relief Committee. The different depots were now being closed wherever the number of applicants fell below 50. On the roads about Puruliá the number had fallen in a fortnight from 1400 to 500, and at the depots the applicants for gratuitous relief had diminished from 2000 to 400.

Agricultural Population.—The Deputy Commissioner has furnished me with no particulars regarding the proportion of agriculturists to labourers. But the Census Report of 1872 (p. cxxxvi.) returns the total "Agricultural and Pastoral Castes" (Hindus) of the Mánbhúm District at 213,688, including males, females, and children; but exclusive of the Musalmáns who follow agriculture, and aboriginal or semi-aboriginal tribes partly living by cultivation. By analysing the details of population arranged according to occupation (pp. clxv.–clxxix.), I find that the total male adults of class iv., *i.e.*, persons engaged in agriculture or with animals, is 170,747. Allowing two other persons as an average for women and children connected with each male adult, the total population living by agriculture or in connection with animals amounts to 512,241. Deducting 1950 males for the "excepted classes" explained at a foregoing page, *i.e.*, persons possessing estates or otherwise well off, a balance remains of 168,797 males under class iv.; or allowing two other persons to each male adult, a total population of 506,391 souls living by husbandry or employed in connection with animals, or tenure-holders belonging to classes who are often people in a small way. This may be taken as the *gross* agricultural population. The total number of male adult "cultivators" as returned by the Census is 163,917, or taking the average of two persons to each male adult as women and children, a *net* agricultural population of 491,751.

The male adults employed in cultivation form about one-third of the total males in the District, and the total number of males, females, and children living by cultivation (as estimated by allowing two other persons to each male adult) amounts to 491,751, or about one-half of the total population of the District (995,570).

Labouring Population.—The Census Report in its Statement of Castes and Nationalities (pp. cxxxiv.–cxxxvii.) returns the labouring classes, below the rank of artisans, of the Mánbhúm District, as follows:—

1. Aborigines	232,777
2. Semi-Hinduised aboriginals	220,648

3. Personal servant castes	26,773
4. Weaver castes	16,528
5. Labouring castes	10,937
6. Boating and fishing castes	5,905
7. Musician and vagabond castes	775
8. Unspecified, Vaishnavs, &c.	16,548
Total ...	530,891

Turning to the Statement of Occupations (pp. clxv.-clxxix.), I find the following numbers under their respective classes. I only take those who may fairly be considered in the rank of labouring men:—

		MALE ADULTS.
Class I. (*Government employ*)	Píyádás	42
Class II. (*Professionals*)	Musicians	1,090
Class III. *Service.*	Personal servants ...	3,895
	Sweepers	64
	Unspecified	3,094
	Water-carriers ...	6
Class V. *Conveyance of goods.*	Cartmen	150
	Palki-bearers	1,144
	Boatmen	47
Class VI. *Poorer craftsmen.*	Brick-makers	2
	Lime-burners	24
	Basket-makers ...	1,252
	Cotton-spinners ...	2,805
	Cotton-carders ...	16
Class VII. *Miscellaneous.*	Beggars	3,397
	Labourers	66,379
	Unemployed	2,339
	Total ...	85,746

The total population of the District is 995,570. Taken by castes, therefore, there are 530,891 persons belonging to labouring classes, or about five-ninths of the total population. According to occupation, there are 85,746 male adults who may fairly be considered in the rank of labouring men, or 257,238 males, females, and children, being above one-fourth of the total population. The discrepancies between the results obtained from the

Caste and Occupation Statements probably arise from the fact that a large proportion of the aboriginal and semi-aboriginal castes (who are here entered as labourers) are in reality cultivators. But they form the lowest class of husbandmen, and on the approach of famine abandon their fields to seek hired labour, and are thus thrown on the labouring population.

The foregoing calculations give, therefore, the following results:—

1. Total population 995,570
2. Agriculturists (Hindus) according to caste statement 213,688
3. Agriculturists (total) according to occupation statement 506,391
4. Labourers (Hindus, aborigines, &c.) according to caste statement 530,891
5. Labourers (total) according to occupation ... 257,238
6. Total of agriculturists and labourers (Hindus and aborigines) according to caste statement 744,579
7. Total of agriculturists and labourers (all) according to occupation 763,629

N.B.—It must be remembered that the total of agriculturists and labourers, according to occupation, is obtained by multiplying the number of *male adults* by three.

PRESIDENCY DIVISION.

24 PARGANAS DISTRICT.

Famine Prices.—The great famine of 1866 did not very seriously affect the 24 Parganás. The Collector in his report to me, dated March 1871, stated that the price of rice in ordinary use among the people in 1866, was Rs. 6 a maund, and of paddy, Rs. 2-8 a maund. The Report of the Famine Commissioners shows that at Mitraganj, where the famine was sharpest, the maximum price of rice was Rs. 5-11 a maund, or 7 seers per rupee. The price of rice at Mitraganj for each month of 1866 are returned as under in the Famine Commissioners' Report :—January and February, 9 seers per rupee; March and April, 8 seers; May, 7½ seers; June and July, 7 seers; August, September, and October, 7½ seers; and November and December, 13 seers per rupee. In 1871 local prices had returned to their ordinary rates before the famine.

History of the Famine.—The following brief account of the famine of 1866 in the 24 Parganás is condensed from the "Report of the Famine Commissioners," vol. i. pp. 350-361 :—The first symptoms of distress were noticed in October 1865, and on the 31st of that month the District Superintendent of Police reported to the Collector that he had "observed very palpable signs of great distress amongst the people in consequence of the failure of the rice crop owing to want of rain;" adding, "It is impossible to disguise the fact that the distress which now prevails is only the commencement of what promises to be a famine." The distress was worst in the north-east of the District, and places were named in which the rice crop had entirely failed. Rice was reported all over the District to be selling at double the rates which prevailed at the same time in the preceding year, and the price was rising rapidly. Thefts increased, in many of the cases only food being taken. It was estimated that, if rain were to fall, the out-turn of the crop would not be above half that of an ordinary year; if no rain should fall, the out-turn would not be above one-eighth. The result of the inquiries made by the Magistrate was that a failure of half the crop was expected; that in some places the people were selling their ornaments and brass vessels. With regard to one subdivision, it was anticipated that "while actual distress will not be general, individual cases of extreme distress will be numerous;" and as to another that "distress will be generally felt, but not acute distress, except in individual cases."

In May 1866, the Collector was authorised to begin relief works on certain roads in the southern part of the District, if any need for employment should arise. Acute and general distress first made itself apparent in that month; a great increase in crime in the south of the District rendered additional police necessary. An inquiry into the state of the Diamond Harbour Subdivision disclosed great suffering; many people were living on leaves and roots of the plantain tree; and the grain which had been reserved for sowing was being consumed. In the Sátkhirá Subdivision prices rose from 12½ seers per rupee on the 16th May till the middle of June, when the price suddenly sprang up to 8 *seers* for the rupee, or Rs. 5 a maund. Money and rice were freely distributed to the famishing—an average of 233 people being relieved daily during August at the Kalároá relief depots.

At a meeting held at Alípur on the 26th July a mixed committee of official and non-official gentlemen was appointed, who at once raised a subscription, and applied to the Board of Revenue for a grant of Rs. 10,000. They resolved to adopt the system of out-door relief; the relieving officer first ascertaining the requirements of different families, and giving tickets entitling the holders to receive a sum of money calculated to support them for a month. Relief Committees were also organised by private native gentlemen with great success. In August it became necessary to import rice into the District. Six hundred maunds of rice were bought at Kushtiá for the Relief Committee, and sent to Kálpí, south of Diamond Harbour, through the Sundarbans. At the end of August the daily number of paupers relieved in the south of the District was about 220 at Kálpí and Ságar Island, 70 at Diamond Harbour, and 113 in the Centres under the control of the Native Committee. The Commissioner of the Division proceeded on a tour of inspection through the afflicted tracts in October, and reported as follows :—"From what we heard and saw, it might be generally stated that throughout this tract the classes who ordinarily live by daily labour and wages, as well as those who live on alms, are now subsisting, not on rice, but on the roots of the *bankachu* (a kind of wild yam), and the leaves of the *sajina*, tamarind, and other trees boiled down. Nevertheless, there was not that universal appearance of attenuation among the people which might have been expected. Almost every labouring man whom we met complained that no work was to be got; the prospect of work universally received with delight, and with an urgent request that it might be immediate."

The Commissioner directed the immediate commencement of works at as many places as possible, on three or four lines of road running through the distressed tract, and authorised the Magistrate to undertake any other work which he could devise. A sum of Rs. 10,000, which remained unused from the grant to the Nadiyá District for works, was placed at the disposal of the Magistrate. In the meantime, the Public Works Department had supplied employment for all who wanted it, on the embankments and roads of the Diamond Harbour Subdivision. In the week ending the 14th July, 2360 were at work daily. The fall of the rains, however, brought the embankment repairs to a close, and the number of labourers employed by the Public Works Department fell gradually to about three hundred daily, at which number it remained throughout the rainy season. The discontinuance of the Works enhanced the distress at first; but the reaping of the early crops gave employment for some weeks; and such work as the Relief Committee could provide was going on. The cessation of agricultural operations in September, however, threw the people out of employment again, and an increase in the number of applicants for gratuitous relief immediately took place. A general fall in the price of grain took place in November, the cheapest sort selling at Rs. 3 a maund at the end of that month, in consequence of importations from the Eastern Districts, and of some of the local cold weather crop being already in the market. During the month operations were contracted at all the relief centres, and on the 24th November six centres in the tract immediately south of Calcutta were closed altogether.

The number of relief centres opened throughout the District

was nineteen, and the numbers relieved on the first day of each month were as follows:—1st July, 264; 1st August, 1162; 1st September, 3156; 1st October, 8862; and 1st November, 9490; after which the number fell with extraordinary rapidity, till all relief was discontinued on the 1st December. The total disbursements are thus reported by the Collector:—Money relief, Rs. 42,043; purchase of food, Rs. 14,004; clothing and miscellaneous, Rs. 1993; total, Rs. 58,040. Out of the special grant of Rs. 10,000 assigned to the Magistrate for the relief works, about Rs. 7000 were expended; employment was given on nine roads over an aggregate length of thirty-four miles; and the aggregate daily total of those thus employed was 31,876.

The mortality in the 24 Parganás from direct starvation was very small. The Famine Committee's Report states that only in two localities (Sátkhirá and Harinábhí) were deaths of residents of the District reported to have been directly attributable to starvation. In this, as in other Districts, the high price of food reduced people to a condition in which they readily succumbed to attacks of diarrhœa and dysentery, which thus took the place of actual starvation. The instances in which death directly proceeded from emaciation and want of food were mostly among people from Orissa and Midnapur, who came across the river on their way to Calcutta, or who wandered about the District in search of employment. Many of these were in such a state of emaciation when they arrived, as to be beyond the hope of recovery.

FAMINE WARNINGS.—The Collector is of opinion that prices reach famine rates when ordinary coarse rice is selling at Rs. 3-12 a maund. The *average* earnings of a day labourer may be estimated at 2½ annas a day; but to maintain himself, wife, and child, he would require at least two seers of rice daily, which, at the rate mentioned above, would cost him three annas, or half an anna a day more than his average daily earnings. He could, however, manage to reduce the quantity of rice somewhat, without suffering actual hunger. In ordinary seasons the average price of such rice is about Rs. 1-14 a maund, and the labourer is able to buy his daily two seers of rice for about 1½ annas. If the price of coarse rice were to rise as high as Rs. 2-8 a maund, or 16 seers per rupee in January, just after the reaping of the winter rice crop, it would indicate the approach of a very severe scarcity, if not of actual famine, later in the year. The principal crop of the District is the *aman*, or winter rice; and although *aus* or autumn rice is largely cultivated in the northern part of the District, it would not make up for an almost total loss of the former.

MEANS OF TRANSIT.—The means of communication in the 24 Parganás are sufficient to avert the extremity of famine by means of importation from other parts of the country. No part of the District is in any danger of absolute isolation in time of scarcity, although there is much room for improvement in the means of internal communication. The Deputy Collector suggests the following as remedial measures against the occurrence of future famines, or to mitigate their severity:—(1.) The collection of District Agricultural Statistics, &c.; (2.) Returns of rainfall, and of exportation and importation of food grains; (3.) Improvement of land tenures, and the opening of model farms illustrating the benefits to be derived from manuring, irrigation, &c.; (4.) The complete drainage of the District, and improvement in the means of internal communication; (5.) The establishment of institutions for the support of persons physically incapable; (6.) Enactment of laws for the more equitable distribution of the profits of land between tenants and landlords, and of the profits of business between capitalists and labourers; (7.) Re-institution of the *panchayat* system, which might act as relief committees in times of distress. Several of these proposed remedies have already been carried out. Others are of a visionary character. But they show how the question strikes the educated native mind.

AREA; OUT-TURN OF CROPS, &c.—The District was surveyed between December 1846, and September 1851. Its area, as then ascertained, exclusive of Calcutta, the Suburbs, and the Sundarbans, amounted to 1,437,440 acres, or 2246 square miles (as against its present area of 2536 square miles). Of the area in 1851, 878,528 acres, or 1372·70 square miles, were returned as under cultivation; 200,512 acres, or 313·30 square miles, as fallow and cultivable; and 358,400 acres, or 560 square miles, as village sites, roads, rivers, jungle, &c. Since the date of the survey, however, the area of the District has been considerably extended by the transfer of several Fiscal Divisions from Nadiyá to the 24 Parganás in 1863. In October 1871, the Surveyor-General reported the revised area of the District, exclusive of the Sundarbans, to be 2536 square miles. The Collector reports to me that no means exist of forming even an estimate of the comparative acreage under the different crops. Statistics collected by the Board of Revenue for 1868-69 return the area under rice cultivation alone at 884,118 acres, or 1381·43 square miles. Such statistics proceed on a loose basis; but so far as they go, they show, when taken along with the return of 1851, that more than half the area of the District is under actual crops. The Collector states that a fair out-turn of paddy from lands paying a rental of Rs. 1-8 and Rs. 3 a *bigha* respectively, would be 10 and 15 maunds, value Rs. 7 and Rs. 12 respectively. Very little rice land in the 24 Parganás pays so high a rent as Rs. 3 per *bigha*. A second crop of oil seeds or pulses is generally taken from *aus* lands; average produce 2½ maunds, value Rs. 5. A second crop of the same kind, and of about the same value, is also obtained from jute land.

AGRICULTURAL POPULATION.—The Collector of the District has not furnished me with any statistics regarding the proportion of agriculturists to labourers, but the Census Report of 1872 in the Statement of Castes and Nationalities (pp. cxviii., cxix.) gives the total "Agricultural and Pastoral Castes" (Hindus) of the 24 Parganás, exclusive of Calcutta, its suburbs, and the shipping, at 265,628, including males, females, and children; but exclusive of Muhammadans and semi-Hinduised aborigines partly or wholly living by agriculture. Analysing the details of population arranged according to occupation (pp. cxli.–clvii.), I find that the total male adults of class iv., *i.e.*, persons engaged in agriculture or with animals, amounts to 329,930. Allowing two other persons as an average for women and children connected with each male adult, the total population living by agriculture or by tending animals amounts to 989,790. Deducting 24,717 male adults for the "excepted classes" explained at a foregoing page, *i.e.*, persons possessing estates or otherwise well off, and for the agricultural labourers whom I have entered under the labouring population, a balance remains of 305,213 males under class iv., or allowing two other persons to each male adult as before, a total population of 915,639 souls living by actual husbandry or by tending animals, or tenure-holders belonging to classes who are often people in a small way. This may be taken as the *gross* agricultural population. The total number of male adult "cultivators," as returned by the Census, is 288,960, or allowing an average of two persons to each male adult as women and children, a total *net* cultivating population of 866,880.

The male adults employed in cultivation form about two-sevenths of the total males in the District; and the total number of males, females, and children living by cultivation (as obtained by allowing two other persons to each male adult), amounts to 866,880, or more than three-sevenths of the total population of the 24 Parganás, exclusive of Calcutta, its suburbs, and the shipping (1,951,137).

LABOURING POPULATION.—The Census Report in its Statement of Castes and Nationalities (pp. cxiv.–cxxiii.), returns the labouring classes, below the rank of artisans, of the twenty-four Parganás, exclusive of Calcutta, &c., as follows:—

1. Aborigines ...	3,325
2. Semi-Hinduised aboriginals ...	251,456
3. Personal servant castes ...	45,325
4. Weaver castes ...	43,968
5. Labouring castes ...	816
6. Boating and fishing castes ...	317,163
7. Musician and vagabond castes ...	849
8. Unclassified, Vaishnavs, &c. ...	44,597
Total ...	707,499

Turning to the Statement of Occupation (pp. cxli.–clvii.), I find the following numbers under their respective classes. I only take those who may fairly be considered in the rank of labouring men:—

		MALE ADULTS.
Class I. (*Government employ*)	Píyádás ...	1,064
Class II. (*Professionals*)	Musicians ...	1,089
Class III. *Service.*	Personal servants ...	11,549
	Sweepers ...	278
	Water-carriers ...	279
	Unspecified ...	10,125
Class IV. *Agriculture, &c.*	Agricultural labourers	15,286

Class V. *Conveyance of goods.*	Cartmen	2,181
	Bullock-drivers ...	320
	Palki-bearers ...	4,752
	Coolies	77,216
	Boatmen	27,232
Class VI. *Poorer sorts of craftsmen.*	Brick-makers ...	1,345
	Lime-burners ...	381
	Coolies	55
	Cane-workers ...	237
	Mat-makers ...	417
	Cage-makers ...	26
	Basket-makers ...	1,009
	Cotton-weavers ...	5,459
	Shoe-makers ...	1,304
	Cotton-carders ...	114
	Spinners	382
	Bird-catchers ...	196
Class VII. *Miscellaneous.*	Beggars and paupers	6,988
	Unemployed ...	18,352
	Total ...	187,636

The population of the District, exclusive of Calcutta, suburbs, and the shipping, is 1,951,137. Taken by castes, therefore, there are 707,499 persons belonging to the labouring classes, or about three-eighths of the total population. According to occupation, there are 187,636 male adults, or 562,908 males, females, and children, comprising above two-sevenths of the total population. The discrepancy between the results obtained from the Caste and Occupation Statements probably arises from the fact that a portion of the semi-aboriginal tribes and the boating and fishing castes (here entered by caste as labourers), are in reality cultivators or fishermen. The semi-aboriginals are often poor and improvident, and on the approach of a famine, many abandon their fields to seek hired labour, and are thus thrown on the labouring population.

The foregoing calculations yield the following results:—

1. Total population 1,951,137
2. Agriculturists (Hindus) according to caste statement 265,628

3. Agriculturists (total) according to occupation	915,639
4. Labourers (Hindus and aborigines) according to caste statement	707,499
5. Labourers (total) according to occupation	562,908
6. Total agriculturists and labourers (Hindus and aborigines) according to caste ...	973,127
7. Total agriculturists and labourers (all) according to occupation	1,478,547

N.B.—It must be remembered that the total of agriculturists and labourers, according to occupation, is obtained by multiplying the *male adults* by three.

NADIYA DISTRICT.

Famine Prices.—The highest price to which rice has risen in Nadiyá District within the last thirty years, excepting in the famine year of 1866, was in 1860, when it rose as high as Rs. 2-12 a maund. The high rates of 1860 were caused by the floods of 1859. The only real famine which has occurred in Nādiyá District within the recollection of the present generation took place in 1866, when the price of rice rose as high as 8 seers per rupee, or Rs. 5 a maund. The Collector in his report to me, dated February 1871, quoted the then current price of common rice to be Rs. 1-14 a maund, and paddy Re. 1 a maund. In 1871 prices had not returned to what were considered ordinary rates before the famine.

History of the Famine.—The famine of 1866 was severely felt in Nadiyá, and the following brief account of it is condensed from the Report of the Famine Commissioners printed in 1867:—The cyclone of 1864 had done great damage to the District, sweeping completely across it. A severe drought occurred the following year; and on the 25th October 1865 the Board of Revenue requested the Commissioner of the Presidency Division to report on the state of the rice crops, and the prices of food in each of the Districts under his charge. The Collector of Nadiyá accordingly reported on the 31st October that the out-turn of the rice crop was expected to be less than half that produced in ordinary years; that in some parts of the District the plant was utterly destroyed, so as to be beyond the hope of saving, even in the event of a fall of rain; and the cold-weather crop was also threatened with comparative failure if the drought should continue. The Collector stated that there was a disinclination on the part of the cultivators to pay their rents, on the ground that every pice would be required to buy food, and that he had been asked to establish a fixed rate at which the storekeepers and merchants should be compelled to sell rice. The poorest classes had already implored Government relief, as they were without food. The Collector also submitted the following statement of the prices of food then ruling (31st October 1865), as compared with the rates of the previous year:—*Aus* paddy, rate in 1864, 14 annas a maund; in 1865, Rs. 1-12 a maund: *aus* rice, rate in 1864, Rs. 1-8 a maund; in 1865, from Rs. 2-14 to Rs. 3 a maund: *aman* paddy, rate in 1864, 15 annas a maund; in 1865, Rs. 2 a maund; *aman* rice, rate in 1864, from Rs. 1-8 to Rs. 2-8 a maund; in 1865, from Rs. 2-12 (very bad quality) to Rs. 4 a maund.

These rates became a little easier when the winter crop was reaped, but the distress continued, and in March 1866 the missionaries of the Church Missionary Society addressed the Lieutenant-Governor on the subject. One of these, the Rev. T. G. Lincke, stated that "a certain measure of rice, which some years ago cost three or four pice, now sells at thirteen or fourteen pice, which alone is sufficient to account for the present distress of the poor. Were I to tell you instances of how long many must go without food, and what sort of materials they contrive to convert into food, you could not believe it, for it is really incredible, and yet is true nevertheless." Another missionary, the Rev. F. Schurr of Kápásdángá, stated that "respectable farmers are so much reduced in circumstances that they cannot employ nearly so many day labourers as they used to do in former times, and consequently the labouring classes are reduced to the point of starvation. They are now (March 1866) able to glean a little wheat, grain, &c.; but after a month all the crops will have been gathered in, when nothing can be obtained by gleaning in the fields. They are now thrown upon roots, berries, &c., for their chief support, and when that supply is exhausted, they will be forced to eat the rind of trees, grass, &c. I never witnessed such misery in my life."

This appeal of the missionaries resulted in a report being called for from the Collector, on the condition of the poor in Nadiyá District in general, and of the Christian villages alluded to in particular. A thorough inquiry was then made, from which it appeared that the distress was severest in the central divisions of the District, while in those parts in which much of the land is devoted to date-trees, chilies, tobacco, and other of the more lucrative crops, the distress was least felt. The Collector, on the 30th April 1866, reported that the suffering was much less in the neighbourhood of Kushtiá, Chuádángá, and Mihrpur than in other parts. "Regarding the rest of the District," the Collector stated, "all accounts agree that there is great distress. There is no famine (*sic*), for grain is to be had, but there is very little money to buy it at the prevailing prices. For some months the poor (and in this word I include almost all the working classes) have not had more than one meal a day, and it is to be feared that many have not had even that. Nor can there be any doubt that there is a good deal of illness; and I am afraid there have already been a few deaths owing to want of sufficient food for so long. Here in Krishnagar the poor have been in the habit of going daily in numbers to the houses of the upper and middle classes of natives at the time of the evening meal, in order to get whatever food might be left over." In the Collector's opinion the time had then come for Government to alleviate the distress by giving employment to the people in road-making and other relief works; and the Government authorised him to devote the sum of Rs. 20,000 out of an available local fund of Rs. 45,000 for such works.

In May, public meetings were held at Krishnagar, Ránághát, Bangáon, and Chuádángá, and subscriptions raised for the relief of the sufferers. Relief depots were opened at several places in Krishnagar, where uncooked rice was gratuitously distributed. Small sums of money were sent out to the subdivisions to meet cases of immediate want; and the Relief Committee determined to import rice from Kushtiá and Calcutta for local sale, this course being thought more beneficial than grants of money, which would only have the effect of raising the selling price of grain in the different localities. Before the end of May, relief works had been started at different parts in most of the subdivisions, and a sum of Rs. 5000 was assigned to the District by Government from the unexpended balance of the North-West Provinces Famine Fund. In June the distress became very severe, and the money was rapidly expended both in giving employment to those who could work, and in feeding those who could not. On the 18th June the Commissioner roughly calculated that about two thousand five hundred persons were employed on the special relief works, and that on public works of all kinds nearly four thousand persons were employed. More money was applied for, and on the 20th June the Collector received another Rs. 5000, and further sums from time to time. In August another sum of Rs. 30,000 was granted for relief works under the Magistrate's superintendence, and Rs. 20,000 were spent. Feeding depots were established at different places, and in a few instances allowances made to a limited number of people at their own homes. Weaving work was also found for the weaving caste in Krishnagar, and this measure is stated to have been even financially successful, no loss having occurred. The result of the various measures adopted was, that deaths by actual starvation and all mortality beyond that inseparable from a period of unusual scarcity were averted. The total amount raised by local subscriptions was about Rs. 11,000, while Government contributed Rs. 24,500.

In some parts of the District the distress caused by the drought was greatly aggravated by inundation. The rivers began to rise early in July with unprecedented rapidity, and the floods did much injury to the early (*aus*) rice crop in the western part of the District, along the banks of the Bhágirathí. Before the actual extent of the damage was ascertained, the floods had caused a panic in certain tracts, and the price of rice rose to two and a half annas per seer, or Rs. 6-4 a maund. It was reported by the Commissioner that about eighteen thousand acres of rice and over two thousand acres of indigo had been submerged, and the crops almost totally destroyed. The state of the people in the inundated tract was deplorable; they fed on the leaves of trees and roots of wild plants. Fifteen thousand persons were estimated to be suffering from want of food in this tract of country.

The general distress began to diminish in August. The Commissioner, who visited the District during that month, returned the price of rice in different places to be as follows:—At Kushtiá, from Rs. 3-14 to Rs. 4 per maund; at Chuádángá, Rs. 4-5 a maund; and at Krishnagar, from Rs. 4-12 to Rs. 5 per maund. The *aus* or early rice crop, which is extensively grown in Nadiyá, found its way into the market at the end of this month, and in parts which had escaped inundation the turn-out was usually good. Prices fell rapidly, and a few relief centres in the interior of the District were closed as being no longer required. In the beginning of September the Collector and Committee took measures towards gradually contracting the relief operations. All able-bodied labourers were drafted off to the relief works; and with regard to the rest the daily relief was gradually reduced, so as to offer no temptation to those who could support themselves. The number of applicants rapidly fell off, and in October only three or four relief centres remained open in the part of the District which had suffered most.

Throughout the whole District twenty-four principal centres of relief were, at one time or another, in operation; besides about sixteen minor centres, at which private gentlemen aided the Committee by distributing food at their residences, in localities remote from any principal centre.

"The aggregate of the daily numbers who received gratuitous relief throughout the operations is returned by the Collector at 601,123." The average number daily employed during the last week of May was 550; during the last week of June, 4415; during the last week of July, 12,059; during the last week of August, 5163; during the last week of September, 460. "The aggregate of the daily number employed on relief works was 337,059," including those employed up to February 1867. Relief works were suspended on the 10th October 1866, but it was found necessary to resume them on the 5th November, as the reaping of the cold-weather crop did not afford so much employment as was expected. The expenditure on these works up to October was about Rs. 33,000, and about Rs. 15,000 afterwards; total, Rs. 48,000. The total amount expended on gratuitous relief was Rs. 35,488, of which Rs. 24,500 were assigned by Government, and Rs. 10,988 raised by private subscription within the District. The following is an extract from the report of the Collector of the District upon the relief works carried on:—"These works consisted of repairs and construction of roads, tanks, and embankments. The first object was to provide employment for those in distress, without requiring them to go to any great distances from their houses; and that being carefully borne in mind, the next object was to get as good a return for the expenditure as possible. It happened that there was a good field for improvement at each of the principal centres of distress, so that no money was expended in one place which I should have preferred to spend at another. No wholesale contractors were employed; the workpeople were paid direct, generally by daily wages, which varied according to sex and age, from three pice to ten pice; payments were also sometimes made by taskwork. Payment in food was attempted once or twice, but it was found that private charitable relief gave quite enough in that respect, and money payments prevailed everywhere." The Collector estimates the return of work at one-half of the quantity which would have been obtained had none but able-bodied labourers been employed. Allowing, therefore, Rs. 24,000 of the Rs. 48,000 spent on relief works to be counted as charity, and adding the Rs. 35,488 expended on gratuitous relief, the total cost of relief during the famine amounted to Rs. 59,488, of which sum Government defrayed Rs. 48,508. The relief given to the distressed was timely and sufficient; and, as stated, there is every reason to believe that little mortality occurred beyond the inevitable diseases in times of scarcity. Valuable co-operation and assistance were rendered to the District Officers by European and Native gentlemen throughout the District.

FAMINE WARNINGS.—The Collector, in his report to me of February 1871, states that prices should be considered to have reached famine rates when the cheapest sort of rice sells at eleven seers per rupee, or Rs. 3-10 a maund.

This estimate is made on a calculation of the earnings of the lowest class of labourers at not less than Rs. 4-8 per month—a rate only sufficient to maintain the family in food and clothing, and to keep a roof over their heads in ordinary seasons. With rice at the price mentioned, this sum would just save him and his family from absolute starvation. The smaller agriculturists, however, would be thrown on the market as labourers, while the general increase of prices would have narrowed the demand for labour. Wages would fall, and if, as is likely, they sank below Rs. 4 a month, the labouring population would begin to starve. With rice at Rs. 3-5 per maund, *i.e.*, twelve seers to the rupee, the lesser agriculturists could probably hold on for one season, and maintain themselves by loans on the future produce of their lands. The loss of crops in any season, or a serious rise in prices after the harvesting of the winter crops, or in January or February, would, in the opinion of the Collector, be warnings of famine. The cheapest sort of rice selling at eighteen seers for the rupee, or Rs. 2-3-6 per maund, in January, would be a warning of the approach of famine later in the year.

The Collector thinks that a good test of the state of the people is the condition of the excise, especially that arising from the cheaper liquors. The greater part of this revenue is derived from the towns; and the Collector states that any calamity which only affects the country without materially affecting the towns does not make itself perceptible through the fluctuations of the excise revenue. An instance of this occurred in 1871, when the tremendous floods had very little effect on the excise, as the towns being on the highlands were scarcely touched by the inundation. Although it proved very destructive to the crops, prices were but little affected, as food was easily procurable from elsewhere. The District chiefly depends on the *aman* or winter harvest; and should the *aus* harvest wholly fail, the winter rice, if an average crop, would suffice to support the population of the District, even if entirely isolated. As matters now stand, prices would not rise to the famine rates if the adjoining Districts had produced an average harvest of both sorts of rice. Nadiyá is in no danger whatever of isolation in the event of a famine; and the means of importation, namely, the railway, the roads, and the rivers, are in the opinion of the Collector abundant. He offers no suggestions as regards remedial or mitigating measures during famine in the District.

AREA; OUT-TURN OF CROPS, &c.—According to the Revenue Survey, the total area of the Nadiyá District was about 3,249·52 square miles, or 2,079,692 acres. Changes, however, have taken place since then, and the Surveyor-General reports the area of the District, as revised up to October 1871, at 3414 square miles. The Collector states that no returns exist showing the proportions of cultivated land, land capable of cultivation but not actually under tillage, and uncultivable land; nor any statistics showing the area under the principal crops. By far the larger portion of the cultivated land, however, is under rice. The Collector estimates a fair yield of the best land to be of paddy five or six maunds per *bigha*—which compared with adjoining Districts seems too low—value Rs. 5 to Rs. 6 per *bigha*. The out-turn of lowest sort of land is from two to two and a half maunds of paddy per *bigha;* the Collector estimating the value of the paddy at from Rs. 2 to Rs. 2-8 a *bigha.* *Aus* land also yields a second crop, such as linseed, wheat, mustard, gram, peas, &c., after the rice crop has been reaped. The out-turn of this second crop is from two or three maunds per *bigha,* and the value from Rs. 4 to Rs. 6 per *bigha.* Lands which grow the *aman* and other descriptions of rice do not yield a second crop. The Collector reports the highest general rate for rice-land to be Rs. 1-4 a *bigha,* and the lowest to be 8 annas a *bigha.* Some old leases show rents to have been as low as from 1½ to 2 annas a *bigha* in the last century.

Agricultural Population.—The Collector has furnished me with no particulars regarding the proportion of agriculturists to labourers. But the Census Report of 1872 (pp. cxviii., cxix.) returns the total "Agricultural and Pastoral Castes" (Hindus) of Nadiyá District at 252,196, including males, females, and children, but exclusive of Musalmáns and semi-Hinduised aborigines living by agriculture. Analysing the details of population arranged according to occupation (pp. cxliv.–cxlvi.), I find that the total male adults of class iv., *i.e.,* persons engaged in agriculture or with animals, is 244,820. Allowing two other individuals as an average for women and children connected with each male adult, the population living by agriculture or by tending animals amounts to 734,460. Deducting 6096 male adults for the "excepted classes" explained at a previous page, *i.e.,* persons possessing estates or otherwise well off, a balance remains of 238,724 males under class iv.; or allowing two other persons to each male adult, a total population of 716,172 living by husbandry or employed in connection with animals, or tenure-holders belonging to the classes who are generally people in a small way. This may be taken as the *gross* agricultural population. The total number of male adult "cultivators" as returned by the Census is 231,459, or allowing an average of two persons to each male adult as women and children, a total *net* agricultural population of 694,377.

The male adults employed in cultivation form about one-fourth of the total males in the District; and the total number of males, females, and children living by cultivation (as obtained by allowing two other persons to each male adult) amounts to

694,377, or about three-eighths of the total population of the District (1,812,795).

LABOURING POPULATION.—The Census Report, in its Statement of Castes and Nationalities (pp. cxiv.–cxxviii.), returns the labouring classes, below the rank of artisans, of the Nadiyá District thus:—

1. Aboriginal tribes	789
2. Semi-Hinduised aborigines	179,213
3. Personal servant castes	38,310
4. Weaver castes	37,834
5. Labouring castes	929
6. Boating and fishing castes	54,669
7. Musician and vagabond castes	1,789
8. Unspecified, Vaishnavs, &c.	32,036
Total ...	345,569

Turning to the Statement of Occupation (pp. cxli.–clvi.), I find the following numbers under their respective classes. I only take those who may be fairly considered in the rank of labouring men:—

		MALE ADULTS.
Class I. (*Government employ*)	Píyádás	1,858
Class II. (*Professionals*)	Musicians ...	2,504
Class III. *Service.*	Personal servants	8,179
	Sweepers	496
	Water-carriers ...	17
	Unspecified ...	7,096
Class V. *Conveyance of goods.*	Cartmen ...	1,101
	Bullock-drivers	108
	Palki-bearers ...	6,156
	Boatmen ...	5,926
Class VI. *Poorer sorts of craftsmen.*	Mat-makers ...	1,086
	Diggers	5
	Basket-makers ...	1,009
	Cotton-carders ...	22
	Cotton-spinners ...	95
	Cotton-weavers	13,680
	Shoe-makers ...	684
	Cane-weavers ...	267

Class VII. *Miscellaneous.*	Beggars ...	10,106
	Labourers ...	101,843
	Unemployed ...	9,133
	Total ...	171,371

The total population of the District is 1,812,795. Taken by castes, therefore, there are 345,569 persons belonging to the labouring classes, or about one-fifth of the total population. According to occupation, there are 171,371 male adults, who may be considered in the rank of labouring men, or 514,113 males, females, and children, comprising two-seventh part of the total population.

The foregoing calculations give the following results :—

1. Total population	1,812,795
2. Agriculturists (Hindus) according to caste statement	252,196
3. Agriculturists (total) according to occupation statement	716,172
4. Labourers (Hindus, aborigines, &c.) according to caste statement	345,569
5. Labourers (total) according to occupation statement	514,113
6. Total of agriculturists and labourers (Hindus, aborigines, &c.) according to caste statement	597,765
7. Total of (all) agriculturists and labourers according to occupation statement ...	1,230,285

N.B.—It must be remembered that the total of agriculturists and labourers, according to occupation, is obtained by multiplying the number of male adults by three.

JESSOR DISTRICT.

FAMINE PRICES.—The maximum price for common rice in Jessor District during the Bengal Famine of 1866, is returned by the Collector in his report to me in 1871, to have been Rs. 4 per maund, or 10 seers for the rupee. Although prices were high, there was no absolute famine in Jessor in 1866. Up to 1871 prices had not returned to their ordinary rates.

FAMINE WARNINGS.—The Collector states that there has been no actual famine in the District within the experience of the present generation, and he finds it difficult to speculate as to what should be considered probable warnings of famine. He thinks that famine may be considered very imminent when coarse rice is selling at Rs. 5 a maund, or 8 seers for the rupee. At these rates, the very poor classes (those below the status of an average cultivator) would have to deny themselves everything beyond very short rations of rice and a little salt, and if the price rose higher than this, they could not manage to exist at all without Government relief. Jessor mainly depends on the *aman* or winter rice harvest; the *aus* or autumn rice crop could not compensate for an almost total loss of the *aman*, or even enable the people to live throughout the year without actual famine.

MEANS OF TRANSIT, &c.—The Collector states that the means of communication by river and road are amply sufficient for importations into any part of the District in times of famine. There is no danger of the isolation of any tract. The only suggestion made by the Collector as regards remedial or mitigating measures during famine is that Government should import rice into the distressed tract.

OUT-TURN OF CROPS. — Great uncertainty attaches to all statistics in Lower Bengal as to the out-turn of crops. The following must be taken only as an approximate estimate; but to avoid error as far as possible, I give returns from two separate sources:—

The Collector, in his special report to me (1871), estimates that a fair out-turn from land paying an annual rent of 9s. an acre or Rs. 1-8 a *bigha*, would be about twelve maunds per *bigha*, the value of which would be about Rs. 6 per *bigha*, besides the straw. On the higher levels, after the *aus* or autumn rice crop has been reaped, the same ground yields a second crop of peas, mustard seed, or til seed. The out-turn of this second crop is reported at about two and a half maunds per *bigha*. For mustard or til seed a fair out-turn would be about two maunds a *bigha*. The average prices for these second crops throughout the year are, for peas Rs. 2-8 a maund; mustard seed, Rs. 3-8 a maund; til seed, Rs. 1-8 a maund. Consequently, a well-situated rice field paying a rent of Rs. 1-8 a *bigha* should, with a cold weather crop of peas, yield a crop of say twelve maunds of paddy, value Rs. 6 besides the straw; and a second one of two and a half maunds of peas, value Rs. 6-4; total Rs. 12-4 per *bigha*. With mustard seed as the second crop, the average value of the out-turn would be Rs. 13 per *bigha;* and with til seed, Rs. 9 per *bigha*. Very little land in Jessor District pays so high a rent as Rs. 3 a *bigha*. The Collector gives an unusually high estimate, namely, that from such land a fair out-turn would be 18 to 20 maunds a *bigha*, value Rs. 12 to Rs. 14. No second crop is obtained from this description of land. The above calculation omits the value of the straw, which in some Districts, where transit by road is dear, is consumed for thatching and the cattle in the homestead, but which in a fluvial District, with cheap water communication like Jessor, fetches a high price.

The following is another estimate by a very able officer in 1870. In that year Mr Collector Westland reported the average produce of an acre (3 *bighas*) of *aman* or one-crop land at from thirty to thirty-five maunds of paddy, of the value from Rs. 22 to Rs. 26. The same gentleman estimates the produce of a *bigha* of *aus* land at twenty-five maunds of paddy, value Rs. 18; besides the second crop; and the produce of an acre of *boro* rice land at from twenty-five to thirty maunds of paddy, valued at from Rs. 18 to Rs. 23. The rent of rice land varies in the different sub-divisions, from 14 annas to Rs. 1-8 a *bigha*.

Agricultural Population.—The Collector of the District does not furnish me with any particulars regarding the proportion of agriculturists to labourers, but the Census Report of 1872 (pp. cxviii., cxix.) in its Statement of Castes and Nationalities gives the total "Agricultural and Pastoral Castes" (Hindus) of the Jessor District at 100,914, including males, females, and children, exclusive of Musulmáns and semi-Hinduised aboriginals living by agriculture. Analysing the details of population arranged according to occupation at pp. cxli.-clvii., I find that the total male adults of class iv., *i.e.*, persons engaged in agriculture or with animals, are 427,020. Allowing two other persons as an average for women and children connected with each male adult, the total population living by agriculture or by tending animals amounts to 1,281,060. Deducting 11,971 male adults for the "excepted classes" explained at a foregoing page, *i.e.*, persons possessing estates, or otherwise well off, a balance remains of 415,049 males under class iv., or allowing two other persons to each, a total population of 1,245,147 souls living by actual husbandry or by tending animals, or tenure-holders belonging to classes who are often people in a small way. This may be taken as the *gross* agricultural population. The total number of male adult "cultivators" as returned by the Census, is 411,811, or allowing an average of two persons to each male adult as women and children, a total *net* cultivating population of 1,235,433.

The total male adults employed in cultivation form about two-fifths of the total males in the District, and the total number of males, females, and children living by cultivation (as obtained by allowing two other persons to each male adult), amounts to 1,235,433, being about three-fifths of the total population, 2,075,021.

LABOURING POPULATION.—The Census Report, in its Statement of Castes and Nationalities, pp. cxiv.–cxxiii., returns the labouring classes, below the rank of artisans, of the Jessor District as follow. Some of the figures have been corrected from the District Census Statements, as subsequently compiled by Mr C. F. Magrath:—

1. Aboriginal tribes	472
2. Semi-Hinduised aboriginals	343,341
3. Personal servant castes	47,399
4. Weaver castes	52,285
5. Labouring castes	693
6. Boating and fishing castes	87,153
7. Musician and vagabond castes	2,125
8. Unclassified, Vaishnavs, &c.	17,605
Total ...	551,073

Turning to the Statement of Occupation, pp. cxli.–clvii., I

find the following numbers under [their respective classes. I only take those who may fairly be considered in the rank of labouring men:—

Class	Occupation	Male Adults.
Class I. (*Government employ*)	Píyádás	87
Class II. (*Professionals*)	Musicians	1795
Class III. *Service.*	Personal servants	12,194
	Sweepers	153
	Water-carriers	3
	Unspecified	7924
Class V. *Conveyance of goods.*	Cartmen	144
	Bullock-drivers	17
	Palki-bearers	4802
	Boatmen	18,315
Class VI. *Poorer sorts of craftsmen.*	Well-diggers	6
	Mat-makers	151
	Basket-makers	143
	Cane-workers	273
	Cotton-spinners	21
	Cotton-weavers	20,009
	Shoe-makers	1253
	Bird-catchers	16
Class VII. *Miscellaneous.*	Beggars	6495
	Labourers	45,539
	Unemployed	5,257
	Total	124,597

The population of Jessor District is 2,075,021. Taken by castes, therefore, there are 551,073 persons belonging to labouring classes, or more than one-fourth of the total population. According to occupation, there are 124,597 male adults, who may fairly be considered in the rank of labouring men, or 373,791 males, females, and children, comprising over one-sixth or the total population. The discrepancies between the results obtained from the Caste and Occupation Statements, probably arise from the fact that a large proportion of the semi-Hinduised aboriginal tribes (who are here entered as labourers) are in reality cultivators. But they form the lowest class of husbandmen, and on the approach of famine abandon their fields to seek hired labour, and are thus thrown on the labouring population.

The foregoing calculations give the following results:—

1. Total population	2,075,021
2. Agriculturists (Hindus) according to caste statement	100,914
3. Agriculturists (total) according to occupation statement	1,245,147
4. Labourers (Hindus and aborigines) according to caste statement	551,073
5. Labourers (total) according to occupation statement	373,791
6. Total of agriculturists and labourers (Hindus, aborigines, &c.) according to caste statement	651,987
7. Total of (all) agriculturists and labourers according to occupation statement ...	1,618,938

N.B.—It must be remembered that the total of agriculturists and labourers, according to occupation, is obtained by multiplying the number of *male adults* by three.

ORISSA DIVISION.

BALASOR DISTRICT.

Famine Prices.—The Orissa Famine of 1866 forms the subject of a special report, and I refrain here from giving more than the bare facts as to what should be considered famine warnings in Orissa, and stating the actual prices reached during the famine of 1866. The famine as it affected Balasor District is very fully recorded at pages 234-256 of the Famine Commissioners' Report (1867) vol. i.

The Collector, in his report to me in 1870, returned the maximum price of rice in Balasor District during the famine of 1866 at Rs. 13 per maund. The Famine Commissioners in their Report give higher rates, and quote prices at Dhámnagar mart in August ranging from one to three seers per rupee. These rates, however, are merely nominal, and indicate that rice was practically not procurable. Any prices above the maximum rates returned by the Collector may be looked upon as nominal.

Famine Warnings.—Local prices have returned to very nearly the same level as before the famine of 1866. The Collector believes that they will never quite do so, as the price of everything has risen, or in other words the purchasing power of money has decreased in Balasor. He considers that the famine of 1866 has ceased to exercise any influence upon the price of food in his District. Thirty-three seers of common husked rice for a rupee may be taken as the average retail price in the month of January. If the price should rise to only sixteen and a half seers per rupee in that month, preparations should at once be made for a famine. Sixteen and a half seers in January would, according to the average rise in prices as the year advances, decrease to twelve and a half in March, eight in May, and probably before the end of July no rice would be left in the District. By that time it would be impossible to import anything by sea till the end of the monsoon. Mr Collector Beams, who has studied the subject very carefully, reports to me that in the event of rice ever rising in January to the rate of sixteen and a half seers per rupee, the higher authorities should be warned of the approach of famine. He believes the whole moral of the terrible calamity of 1866 is, to "get rice into Orissa before the end of March, if there is any serious tightness in January." Among the non-agricultural classes, a hired labourer, with his wife and two children, cannot earn more than Rs. 6 a month. Of this they have to spend as nearly as possible Rs. 3 for rice when it is at thirty-three seers per rupee. The smallest amount that would sustain the working powers of such a family is one and a half maunds of rice a month; and if the price rose to the rate of sixteen and a half seers per rupee, two-thirds of their income would go for the single item of rice alone, calculating that they only ate enough to keep them alive. When rice rises to twelve and a half seers for the rupee, the non-cultivating classes have to begin to do without it. They would naturally betake themselves to split-peas and other pulses. But unfortunately, in Balasor District these crops are scarcely grown. The whole land is under rice, and if rice fails, everything fails.

The agricultural classes would be a little better off, as they would not only start with a store of grain, but be able to prolong the struggle by the sale of their cattle. They would not begin to die till the rains set in. The District depends almost entirely upon its winter rice crop (*sarad*). The autumn crop is insignificant where it is grown at all, and in some Fiscal Divisions it is unknown. It could nowhere make up for the loss of the winter harvest.

The means of importation at the disposal of the District consist of the Orissa trunk road and the seaports. The former is metalled and bridged, except at the larger rivers, which are supplied with good ferry-boats. But the coast of the long land transit is very great. The river ports are five in number, namely, Balasor, Churáman, Chánuyá, Sárathá, Laichanpur, and Subanrekhá, for which see Notification of the Government of Bengal, No. 621, dated 30th March 1858. But none of them are accessible during the southern monsoon, the very season in which a famine would reach its maximum intensity. Hence the imperative duty of the officer in charge of the District, to keep his eye upon the harvests and the state of the markets, and to give timely notice to the higher authorities before the ports are closed in March. It is vain to expect any relief from inland by means of the rivers. They issue from countries which, in times of scarcity, are even worse off than Balasor.

OUT-TURN OF CROPS.—Good land at Re. 1 per STANDARD *bigha* yields 5⅓ to 6⅔ maunds of coarse paddy, and 5 to 5⅔ of fine. Land paying 8 annas a STANDARD *bigha* yields from 3 to 4 maunds. The price of the crop depends on many local circumstances; but a fair average is reported at Rs. 2 for the crop of a STANDARD *bigha* paying a rent of 8 annas, and Rs. 10 for the crop of a STANDARD *bigha* paying Re. 1. Lands lying along the banks of rivers yield a second crop of pulses or oil-seeds such as *Birhi*, *Mug*, *Jara*, and *Sarisha*, averaging 1½ maunds per STANDARD *bigha* worth from Rs. 2 to Rs. 4.

AGRICULTURAL POPULATION.—The Collector has furnished me with no particulars regarding the proportion of agriculturists to labourers. But the Census Report of 1872 (pp. cxxxi., cxxxii.) returns the total "Agricultural and Pastoral Castes (Hindus)" of the Balasor District at 150,590, including males, females, and children, but exclusive of Musalmáns who live by agriculture, and of the semi-aboriginal castes partly living by cultivation. By analysing the details of population arranged according to occupation (pp. clxix., clxx.), I find that the total male adults under class iv., *i.e.*, persons engaged in agriculture or with animals, are 138,693. Allowing two other persons as an average for women and children connected with each male adult, the total population living by agriculture or in connection with animals, amounts to 416,079. Deducting 3698 male adults for the "excepted classes," explained at a foregoing page, *i.e.*, persons possessing estates, or otherwise well off, a balance remains of 134,995 males under class iv.; or allowing two other persons to each male adult, a total population of 404,985 persons living by husbandry or employed in connection with animals, or tenure-holders belonging to classes who are often people in a small way. This is the *gross* agricultural population. The total number of male adult "cultivators" as returned by the Census is 130,000, or taking the average of two persons to each male as women and children, a total *net* agricultural population of 390,000.

The male adults directly employed in cultivation form about one-third of the total males in the District; and the total males, females, and children living by cultivation number 390,000, or just half the total population of the District (770,232).

LABOURING POPULATION.—The Census Report in its Statement of Castes and Nationalities (pp. cxxx.–cxxxiii.) returns the labouring classes, below the rank of artisans, of the Balasor District as follow :—

1. Aborigines	3,699
2. Semi-Hinduised aboriginals	76,334
3. Personal servant castes	30,873
4. Weaver castes	45,078
5. Labouring castes	508
6. Boating and fishing castes	56,482
7. Musician and vagabond castes	1,486
8. Unspecified, Vaishnavs, &c.	23,914
Total ...	238,374

Turning to the Statement of Occupation (pp. clv.–clxxix.), I find the following numbers under their respective classes. I only take those who may fairly be considered in the rank of labouring men :—

Class	Occupation	MALE ADULTS.
Class II. (*Professionals*)	Musicians	800
Class III. *Service.*	Personal servants ...	2,000
	Sweepers	112
	Unspecified	2,657
Class V. *Conveyance of goods.*	Cartmen	162
	Bullock-drivers ...	47
	Palki-bearers ...	878
	Boatmen	175
Class VI. *Poorer craftsmen.*	Brick-makers ...	37
	Lime-burners ...	6
	Mat-makers ...	36
	Basket-makers ...	288
	Cotton-spinners ...	8,299
	Shoe-makers ...	165

Class VII. *Miscellaneous.*	Beggars	6,011
	Labourers	22,609
	Unemployed ...	1,272
	Total ...	45,554

The total population of the District is 770,232. Taken by castes, therefore, there are 238,374 persons belonging to the labouring classes, or about one-third of the total population. According to occupation there are 45,554 male adults who may fairly be considered in the rank of labouring men, or 136,662 males, females, and children, comprising over one-sixth of the total population. The discrepancies between the results obtained from the Caste and Occupation Statements arise from the fact that a large proportion of the semi-aboriginal and weaver castes (who are here entered as labourers) are in reality cultivators. But they form the lowest class of husbandmen, and on the approach of famine abandon their fields to seek hired labour, and are thus thrown on the labouring population.

The foregoing calculations yield the following results:—

1. Total population	770,232
2. Agriculturists (Hindus) according to caste statement	150,590
3. Agriculturists (total) according to occupation statement	404,985
4. Labourers (Hindus, &c.,) according to caste statement	238,374
5. Labourers (total) according to occupation statement	136,662
6. Total (Hindus, &c.,) agriculturists and labourers according to caste statement ...	388,964
7. Total of (all) agriculturists and labourers according to occupation	541,647

N.B.—It must be remembered that the total of agriculturists and labourers, according to occupation, is attained by multiplying the number of *male adults* by three.

CATTACK DISTRICT.

Famine Prices.—A full account of the famine of 1866 in Cattack District is given in vol. i. of the Famine Commissioners' Report, pp. 183–218. The highest price which rice reached during the famine is returned in the Report at Rs. 10 per maund, or 4 seers for the rupee.

The Collector considers that prices reach famine rates when only 10½ seers of common husked rice can be got for a rupee, and that relief operations should then commence. In average seasons, such rice, the universal food of the people, seldom rises above 26 seers for the rupee. If the price of rice in January should reach 20 seers for the rupee, a very severe scarcity or actual famine is to be feared, as the ordinary rate at that time is seldom less than 33 or 34 seers for the rupee. He would accept such a rise of price as a distinct warning of famine, unless it were susceptible of explanation from local or temporary causes. The District depends almost entirely on the *sarad* or winter rice, the acreage under the *biali* or *aus* rice being only one-fourth of that under *sarad*. In the event, therefore, of a general failure of the December harvest, the following one in August and September will not make up for the deficiency. In 1866 the price of common rice rose from 13 seers per rupee in January to 4 in June.

Preventive Works.—Since the famine of 1866 much has been done to prevent a recurrence of a similar calamity. Harbours, canals, and regular steam communication with Calcutta have broken in upon the isolation of Orissa. Irrigation works have also been carried out on an extensive scale. The Collector reports that even what has been already effected would avert the extremity of famine throughout most of the District, by importations *via* False Point and the Dhámrá River. He believes that, upon the completion of the measures now in progress, the recurrence of famine such as that of 1866 will be impossible. The most inaccessible portion of the District at present is the Jájpur Subdivision, and it would be very difficult in the dry season to throw large supplies of grain into it from the sea-coast. In the absence of a canal, the Collector considers it most important that the northern part of this subdivision should be connected with tidal waters by a road.

Out-turn of Crops.—Official records which represent the agricultural state of the District in 1842, return the proportion of cultivated, cultivable, and waste lands as follows:—Under cultivation, 857,482 acres; cultivable, 94,357 acres; jungle and uncultivable, 866,486 acres; total, 1,818,325 acres, excluding 407,086 acres of land of which no detailed measurement had been made. Since then, however, a much larger extent of land has been brought under tillage. According to the Settlement Papers of 1837, the total crop of the District for one year amounted to upwards of six and a half million hundredweight, grown on 670,209 acres. Of this area, 458,696 acres were under rice, the crop of which was estimated at over five million hundredweight. The local *bigha* is 3 times the Bengal one; but a standard *bigha* of two-crop (*Dofasli*) land paying Re. 1 yields one *bharan* of unhusked paddy, or about 4½ maunds worth Rs. 2-3, and also a second crop of *Mug* or *Birhi* of 1½ maunds worth Rs. 2, total value of crop, Rs. 4-3 per standard *bigha*. A (standard) *bigha* of *Sarad*, or single-crop land, paying Re. 1, will grow 8¾ maunds of paddy worth Rs. 4-5. Two-crop land paying half the above rent gives a crop of *Biali* rice and *Mug*, valued at Rs. 1-8, or Rs. 2 per standard *bigha*. The above shows that one-fourth to one-third of the produce is paid as rent, the remaining three-quarters and the straw going to the cultivator for his capital and labour.

Agricultural Population.—The Collector of the District does not furnish me with any particulars regarding the proportion of agriculturists to labourers. But the Census Report of 1872 (pp. cxxxi., cxxxii.) returns the total "Agricultural and Pastoral Castes" (Hindus) of the Cattack District, at 306,848, including males, females, and children; excluding semi-Hinduised aboriginals and Musalmáns, partly or wholly living by agriculture. By analysing the details of population arranged according to occupation at pp. clxix., clxx., I find that the total of male adults under class iv., *i.e.*, persons employed in agriculture or with animals, is 212,248. Allowing two other persons as an average for women and children connected with each male adult, the total population living by agriculture, or in connection with animals, amounts to 636,744. Deducting 6124 male adults for the "excepted classes" explained at a previous page, *i.e.*, persons possessing estates, or otherwise well off, a balance remains of 206,124 males under class iv.; or allowing two other persons to each male adult, a total population of 618,372 souls living by husbandry or employed in connection with animals, or tenure-holders belonging to classes who are often people in a small way. This may be taken as the *gross* agricultural population. The total number of male adult "cultivators" as returned by the Census is 177,885, or taking the average of two persons to each male adult as women and children, a total net cultivating population of 533,655.

The male adults directly employed in cultivation form about one-fourth of the total males in the District; and the total number of males, females, and children living by cultivation amounts to 533,655, or about two-fifths of the total population of the District (1,494,784).

LABOURING POPULATION.—The Census Report in its Statement of Castes and Nationalities (pp. cxxx.–cxxxiii.) returns the labouring classes, below the rank of artisans, of the Cattack District as follows:—

1. Aborigines	19,483
2. Semi-Hinduised aboriginals	195,709
3. Personal servant castes	57,508
4. Weaver castes	57,292
5. Labouring castes	1,931
6. Boating and fishing castes	67,372
7. Musician and vagabond castes	2,848
8. Unclassified, Vaishnavs, &c.	34,183
Total	436,326

Turning to the Statement of Occupation (pp. clv.–clxxix.), I find the following numbers under their respective classes. I only take those who may fairly be considered in the rank of labouring men:—

		MALE ADULTS.
Class II. (*Professionals*)	Musicians	1,623
Class III. *Service.*	Personal servants	9,579
	Sweepers	300
	Unspecified	4,864

Class V. *Conveyance of goods.*	Cartmen	1,537
	Bullock-drivers ...	1,437
	Palki-bearers	2,017
	Boatmen	1,751
Class VI. *Poorer sorts of craftsmen.*	Brick-makers	157
	Lime-burners ...	2
	Mat-makers	421
	Basket-makers ...	1,560
	Cane-workers ...	17
	Cotton-spinners ...	14,449
	Shoe-makers	255
	Cotton-carders ...	186
Class VII. *Miscellaneous.*	Beggars	11,377
	Labourers	69,975
	Unemployed	7,199
	Total ...	128,706

The total population of the Cattack District is 1,494,784. Taken by castes, therefore, there are 436,326 persons belonging to the labouring classes, or about two-sevenths of the total population. According to occupation, there are 128,706 male adults who may fairly be considered in the rank of labouring men, or 386,118 males, females, and children, comprising over one-fourth of the total population. The discrepancy between the results obtained from the Caste and Occupation Statements arises from the fact that a large proportion of the semi-aboriginal and boating and fishing castes (who are here entered as labourers) are in reality cultivators. But they form the lowest class of husbandmen, and on the approach of famine abandon their fields to seek hired labour, and are thus thrown on the labouring population.

The foregoing calculations give the following results:—

1. Total population	1,494,784
2. Agriculturists (Hindus) according to caste statement	306,848
3. Agriculturists (total) according to occupation statement	618,372
4. Labourers (Hindus, &c.) according to caste statement	436,326

5. Labourers (total) according to occupation statement	386,118
6. Total (Hindus, &c.) agriculturists and labourers according to caste statement	743,174
7. Total of (all) agriculturists and labourers according to occupation statement ...	1,004,490

N.B.—It must be remembered that the total of agriculturists and labourers, according to occupation, is obtained by multiplying the number of *male adults* by three.

PURI DISTRICT.

Famine Prices.—The famine in 1866, so far as it affected Purí District, is fully described in the District Narrative, at pp. 219 to 233 of the Report of the Famine Commissioners. The maximum price of rice reached during the famine of 1866 is returned by the Collector at Rs. 7-4 per maund, or 5½ seers per rupee. I have no information before me as to the point at which famine price may be held to be reached, or as to what rate in January or February should be taken as a warning of the approach of famine later in the year.

Agricultural Population.—The Collector has furnished me with no particulars regarding the proportion of agriculturists to labourers. But the Census Report of 1872 (pp. cxxxi., cxxxii.) returns the total "Agricultural and Pastoral Castes" (Hindus) of the Purí District at 317,479, including males, females, and children; but exclusive of Musalmáns who live by agriculture, and of the aboriginal and semi-aboriginal castes living by cultivation. By analysing the details of population arranged according to occupation (pp. clxix., clxx.), I find that the total male adults under class iv., *i.e.*, persons engaged in agriculture or with animals, is 127,181. Allowing two other persons as an average for women and children connected with each male adult, the total population living by agriculture or in connection with animals amounts to 381,543. Deducting 3369 male adults for the "excepted classes" explained at a foregoing page, *i.e.*, persons possessing estates or otherwise well off, a balance remains of 123,812 males under class iv.; or allowing two other persons to each male adult, a total population of 371,436 souls living by husbandry or employed in connection with animals, or tenure-holders belonging to classes who are often people in a small way. This is the *gross* agricultural population. The total number of male adult "cultivators" as returned by the Census is 113,297, or taking the average of two persons to each male adult for women and children, a total *net* agricultural population of 339,891.

The male adults directly employed in cultivation form about two-sevenths of the total males of the District; and the total number of males, females, and children living by cultivation amounts to 339,891, or about three-sevenths of the total population of the District (769,674).

LABOURING POPULATION.—The Census Report in the Statement of Castes and Nationalities (pp. cxxx.-cxxxiii.) returns the labouring classes, below the rank of artisans, of the Purí District as follows:—

1. Aborigines	16,474
2. Semi-Hinduised aboriginals	88,831
3. Personal servant castes	30,245
4. Weaver castes	20,656
5. Labouring castes	81
6. Boating and fishing castes	30,073
7. Musician and vagabond castes	1,308
8. Unspecified, Vaishnavs, &c.	9,881
Total ...	197,549

Turning to the Statement of Occupations (pp. clv.-clxxix.), I find the following numbers under their respective classes. I only take those who may fairly be considered in the rank of labouring men:—

		MALE ADULTS.
Class II. (*Professionals*)	Musicians ...	752
Class III. *Service.*	Personal servants	2,100
	Sweepers	400
	Unspecified ...	3,734

Class V. *Conveyance of goods.*	Cartmen ...	...	466
	Bullock-drivers	...	348
	Palki-bearers	...	483
	Boatmen ...	...	1,185
Class VI. *Poorer sorts of craftsmen.*	Brick-makers	...	13
	Lime-burners	...	40
	Mat-makers	...	189
	Basket-makers	...	1,104
	Cane-workers	...	77
	Cotton-spinners	...	7,904
	Shoe-makers	...	28
	Cotton-carders	...	122
	Bird-catchers	...	51
Class VII. *Miscellaneous.*	Beggars ...	...	4,535
	Labourers	...	35,645
	Unemployed	...	2,313
	Total	...	61,489

The total population of the District is 769,674. Taken by castes, therefore, there are 197,549 persons belonging to the labouring classes, or above one-fourth of the total population. According to occupation, there are 61,489 male adults who may fairly be considered in the rank of labouring men, or 184,467 males, females, and children, being about one-fourth of the total population. The discrepancy between the results obtained from the Caste and Occupation Statements arises from the fact that a large proportion of the semi-aboriginals, domestic serfs, weavers, and fishing castes (here entered by caste as labourers) are in reality cultivators. But they form the lowest class of husbandmen, and on the approach of famine abandon their fields to seek hired labour, and are thus thrown upon the labouring population.

The foregoing calculations yield the following results:—

1. Total population 769,674
2. Agriculturists (Hindus) according to caste statement 317,479
3. Agriculturists (total) according to occupation statement 371,436
4. Labourers (Hindus, &c.) according to caste statement 197,549

5. Labourers (total) according to occupation statement	184,467
6. Total (Hindus, &c.) agriculturists and labourers according to caste statement ...	515,028
7. Total of (all) agriculturists and labourers according to occupation statement ...	555,903

N.B.—It must be remembered that the total of agriculturists and labourers, according to occupation, is obtained by multiplying the number of male adults by three.

THE END.